The California ELD Standards at a Glance

Horizontal and vertical views enable you to understand how standards change and progress within and across grade levels.

"What the Student Does" sections, which are scannable by proficiency and grade level, spotlight each standard in action.

ELD Standard 1 Organized by Grade Level and Proficiency Level

Standard 1: Exchanging information and ideas

Emerging

K Contribute to conversations and express ideas by asking and answering *yes-no* and *wh-* questions and responding using gestures, words, and simple phrases.

1 Contribute to conversations and express ideas by asking and answering *yes-no* and *wh-* questions and responding using gestures, words, and simple phrases.

2 Contribute to conversations and express ideas by asking and answering *yes-no* and *wh-* questions and responding using gestures, words, and learned phrases.

Expanding

K Contribute to *class, group, and partner discussions by listening attentively, following turn-taking rules*, and asking and answering questions.

1 Contribute to *class, group, and partner discussions by listening attentively, following turn-taking rules*, and asking and answering questions.

2 Contribute to *class, group, and partner discussions, including sustained dialogue, by listening attentively, following turn-taking rules, asking relevant questions, affirming others, and adding relevant information, building on responses, and providing useful feedback.*

Bridging

K Contribute to class, group, and partner discussions by listening attentively, following turn-taking rules, and asking and answering questions.

1 Contribute to class, group, and partner discussions by listening attentively, following turn-taking rules, and asking and answering questions.

2 Contribute to class, group, and partner discussions, including sustained dialogue, by listening attentively, following turn-taking rules, asking relevant questions, affirming others, adding pertinent information, *building on responses, and providing useful feedback.*

Script *in bold italics* indicates content not found in earlier proficiency levels of the same ELD Standard.

Source: *California English Language Development Standards for Grades K–12,* California Department of Education (November 2012).

Notes

Grades K–2 Interacting in Meaningful Ways Collaborative Standard 1

What the **Student** Does

Emerging	Expanding	Bridging

Gist: *Students have conversations with others, follow norms for discussion, and stay on topic through multiple exchanges.*

K They consider:
- Do I contribute to the conversations and express my own ideas?
- Do I ask and answer yes/no questions? Who, what, when, where, why questions?
- Do I use gestures, words, and simple phrases to help others understand what I am saying?

K They *also* consider:
- Do I take part in class, group, and partner discussions?
- Do I listen attentively?
- Do I follow turn-taking rules?
- Do I ask and answer questions?

K Same as Expanding.

Gist: *Students have conversations with classmates and adults, follow norms for discussion, build on one another's ideas, and ask questions.*

1 They consider:
- Do I contribute to the conversations and express my own ideas?
- Do I ask and answer yes/no questions? Who, what, when, where, why questions?
- Do I use gestures, words, and simple phrases to help others understand what I am saying?

1 They *also* consider:
- Do I take part in class, group, and partner discussions?
- Do I listen attentively?
- Do I follow turn-taking rules?
- Do I ask and answer questions?

1 Same as Expanding.

Gist: *Students have conversations with classmates and adults in small and large groups, follow norms for discussion, build on one another's ideas by linking their comments, and ask questions for clarification and explanation.*

2 They consider:
- Do I contribute to the conversations and express my own ideas?
- Do I ask and answer yes/no questions? Who, what, when, where, why questions?
- Do I use gestures, words, and learned phrases to help others understand what I am saying?

2 They *also* consider:
- Do I take part in class, group, and partner discussions with multiple exchanges?
- Do I listen attentively?
- Do I follow turn-taking rules?
- Do I ask relevant questions?
- Do I take time to affirm others (say that I understand their point)?
- Do I add relevant information?

2 They *also* consider:
- Do I help keep the discussion moving forward?
- Do I add to other people's responses?
- Do I let others know when their comments are helpful to me?

Source: *California English Language Development Standards for Grades K–12* (2012).

Gist sections provide digestible synopses for each grade level.

Corresponding CCSS for ELA are displayed for each of the CA ELD Standards so you can better appreciate the alignment between the two sets of standards as the basis for remodeling instructional practice.

CCSS ELA Standards Related to Standard 1 — *Exchanging information and ideas*

Speaking and Listening Standards	Language Standards
K SL.K.1: Participate in collaborative conversations with diverse partners about *kindergarten topics and texts* with peers and adults in small and larger groups. a. Follow agreed-upon rules for discussions (e.g., listening to others and taking turns speaking about the topics and texts under discussion). b. Continue a conversation through multiple exchanges.	**K L.K.1:** Demonstrate command of the conventions of standard English grammar and usage when writing or speaking. a. Print many upper- and lowercase letters. Use frequently occurring nouns and verbs. b. Form regular plural nouns orally by adding /s/ or /es/. c. Understand and use question words (interrogatives). d. Use the most frequently occurring prepositions (e.g., *to, from, in, out, on, off, for, of, by, with*). e. Produce and expand complete sentences in shared language activities.
K SL.K.6: Speak audibly and express thoughts, feelings, and ideas clearly.	**K L.K.6:** Use words and phrases acquired through conversations, reading and being read to, and responding to texts.
1 SL.1.1: Participate in collaborative conversations with diverse partners about *grade 1 topics and texts* with peers and adults in small and larger groups. a. Follow agreed-upon rules for discussions (e.g., listening to others with care, speaking one at a time about the topics and texts under discussion). b. Build on others' talk in conversations by responding to the comments of others through multiple exchanges. c. Ask questions to clear up any confusion about the topics and texts under discussion.	**1 L.1.1:** Demonstrate command of the conventions of standard English grammar and usage when writing or speaking. a. Print all upper- and lowercase letters. b. Use common, proper, and possessive nouns. c. Use singular and plural nouns with matching verbs in basic sentences (e.g., *He hops; We hop*). d. Use personal, possessive, and indefinite pronouns. e. Use verbs to convey a sense of past, present, and future. f. Use frequently occurring adjectives. g. Use frequently occurring conjunctions (e.g., *and, but, or so, because*). h. Use determiners (e.g., articles, demonstratives). i. Use frequently occurring prepositions (e.g., *during, beyond, toward*). j. Produce and expand complete simple and compound declarative, interrogative, imperative, and exclamatory sentences in response to prompts.

CCSS ELA Standards Related to Standard 1 — *Exchanging information and ideas*

continued from previous

Speaking and Listening Standards	Language Standards
1 SL.1.6: Produce complete sentences when appropriate to task and situation. (See grade 1 Language standards 1 and 3 for specific expectations)	**1 L.1.6:** Use words and phrases acquired through conversations, reading and being read to, and responding to texts, including using frequently occurring conjunctions to signal simple relationships (e.g., *because*).
2 SL.2.1: Participate in collaborative conversations with diverse partners about *grade 2 topics and texts* with peers and adults in small and larger groups. a. Follow agreed-upon rules for discussions (e.g., gaining the floor in respectful ways, listening to others with care, speaking one at a time about the topics and texts under discussion). b. Build on others' talk in conversations by linking their comments to the remarks of others. c. Ask for clarification and further explanation as needed about the topics and texts under discussion.	**2 L.2.1:** Demonstrate command of the conventions of standard English grammar and usage when writing or speaking. a. Use collective nouns (e.g., *group*). b. Form and use frequently occurring irregular plural nouns (e.g., *feet, children, teeth, mice, fish*). c. Use reflexive pronouns (e.g., *myself, ourselves*). d. Form and use the past tense of frequently occurring irregular verbs (e.g., *sat, hid, told*). e. Use adjectives and adverbs and choose between them depending on what is to be modified. f. Produce, expand, and rearrange complete simple and compound sentences (e.g., *The boy watched the movie; The little boy watched the movie; The action movie was watched by the little boy*).
	2 L.2.3: Use knowledge of language and its conventions when writing, speaking, reading, or listening. a. Compare formal and informal uses of English.
2 SL.2.6: Produce complete sentences when appropriate to task and situation in order to provide requested detail or clarification. (See grade 2 Language standards 1 and 3 for specific expectations)	**2 L.2.6:** Use words and phrases acquired through conversations, reading and being read to, and responding to texts, including using adjectives and adverbs to describe (e.g., *When other kids are happy, that makes me happy*).

Source: Common Core State Standards, K–12 English Language Arts (2010).

Now that the ELD standard has been unpacked, "What the Teacher Does" provides instructional guidance at each level of proficiency across the grade bands.

Grades K–2 Interacting in Meaningful Ways Collaborative Standard 1

What the **Teacher** Does

During the year, children engage daily in multiple discussions. Discussions occur in pairs, small groups, and with the entire class. Some discussions are adult led. Others are conducted by the children, with teacher guidance and monitoring. Teachers use a variety of structures for discussions and make sure that all children have ample opportunities to contribute, not just the most outspoken children. Furthermore, they ensure that children engage in discussions with diverse partners. That is, children do not always turn to the same one or two neighbors to respond to a prompt or share their thinking.

- **To teach students to contribute to discussions and express ideas:** Teach and demonstrate discussion behaviors that indicate respect for others, such as listening closely, not interrupting, responding to comments, encouraging others to contribute, and acknowledging and appreciating all participants' thinking on the topic.

- **To support students in asking and answering questions:** Use sentence frames with question prompts to demonstrate for students how to ask and answer questions at a variety of depth of knowledge levels. For example, *"How was this similar to . . . ?"* or *"What would happen if . . . ?"* or *"Can you defend your position about . . . ?"*

- **To help students to follow turn-taking:** Use role cards for listening and speaking to teach students how to take turns. For example, a role card with an ear for listening can be created on one side with language frames for listening, such as *"My partner said . . . ,"* can be used. Similarly, a speaking card with a mouth icon printed on one side with a language frame, such as *"I think . . ."* or *"I believe . . . ,"* can be used. In K–2, these role cards can be color coded with speaking in green for go and speak, and red for listening for stop and listen.

- **To demonstrate useful feedback for students:** Engage the children in reflection on the discussion process, such as asking them to consider what was helpful in keeping a discussion on target and what might have made the discussion run more smoothly.

Tips for Differentiation by Proficiency Level

- *Emerging*—Small groups are given images of resources that accompany the day's lesson and are prompted to draw on the images to capture what they learned during the lesson. Use basic sentence frames such as *"I think . . ."* or *"I see. . . ."*

- *Expanding*—Students may respond to sentence frames about the images, such as *"This image shows . . . ,"* *"This image is important because . . . ,"* or *"This image is related . . ."*

- *Bridging*—Students may study images, including photographs and illustrations, and then discuss in small groups or pairs with questions or sentence prompts to guide them.

Note: A variety of sentence frames should be used throughout the school year (notice the variety provided above). ELLs at the Emerging level will need the support of basic frames, but these frames should then be varied according to language purpose throughout the school year. ELLs at the bridging level should then be expected to use more sophisticated sentence frames or to have internalized the language, so that they no longer need them at all. Sentence frames should be used as a scaffold and not a crutch.

Source: 2014 *English Language Arts/English Language Development Framework*, p. 210; video links can be found at https://www.cde.ca.gov/ci/rl/cf/ implementationsupport.asp.

A dedicated academic vocabulary section offers a quick-reference glossary of key words and phrases as they are used within each Standard.

Academic Vocabulary—Key Words and Phrases Related to Standard 1: Exchanging information and ideas

Affirming others: Teacher or student comments that reflect a positive behavior (i.e., turn-taking) or a response or question from someone else in the conversation that exemplifies or clarifies the gist of the discussion.

Asking relevant questions or adding pertinent information: Teacher or student questions and/or comments that move forward the group's understanding of the concepts being studied. These are usually open ended, and can be text dependent, clarifying, and/or making connections questions or comments (to oneself or others, to other texts, to other ideas).

Building on other's responses: Student comments that take into account what others have said in the discussion, and linking their comments to those points.

Collaborative Conversations: Discussing ideas and working jointly with others to develop new thinking.

Multiple exchanges: Discussions where one idea is considered and discussed by several persons, growing richer and more complex as new ideas or examples are added, instead of the typical question/answer, new question/answer pattern that limits discussion.

Providing useful feedback: Offering specific, helpful suggestions to a student in order to improve his or her thinking or work product. Examples include *"You did a good job on _____"* or *"I think you should _____ because it would help _____."*

Speaking audibly: To speak loudly enough to be heard but not so loudly as to be shouting or distorting the message.

Sustained dialogue: Collaborative conversations in which students create new thinking by working with others to add details or further develop thoughts on the topic of discussion.

Turn-taking roles: Various ways for students to consciously listen to others, say their contribution, and then listen again. These roles can include Think-Pair-Share, Reciprocal Teaching, using Equity sticks, etc.

Using learned phrases: Opportunities for students to share their ideas and thoughts by using patterns or prompts to frame their oral language. These can come from pattern drills, sentence frames, and other sources.

Source: Taberski & Burke, (2014), *The Common Core Companion: The Standards Decoded, Grades K–2.*

Notes

Each section concludes with a vignette from the California ELA/ELD Framework, which illustrates standards-based instruction in action.

Example of Practice in Snapshot Related to Standard 1: Exchanging information and ideas

Snapshot 3.4. Collecting and Reporting Data on Litter at School Integrated ELA, ELD, Science, and History–Social Science in Kindergarten

The kindergarteners in Mr. Kravitz's classroom listen to several informational and literary texts about the importance of caring for the environment and the impact litter has on local habitats. Mr. Kravitz guides a discussion about this type of pollution, asking—and encouraging the children to ask—questions about the information they are learning from the texts. He prepares them for paired as well as large-group conversations about what they are learning by revisiting the texts and images and drawing attention to some of the vocabulary that may be particularly useful for their discussions. For example, he reviews and writes on a chart some of the general academic (e.g., *discard, accumulate, observe, impact*) and domain-specific (e.g., *habitat, pollute, litter*) vocabulary from the texts that convey important ideas.

Next he has students meet in pairs to talk about what they have learned. Many of them refer to the chart to remind themselves and each other about the concepts and accompanying vocabulary. After sharing in pairs, the children gather in small groups to draw and label illustrations about what they learned and discussed. They work collaboratively, talking about their understandings and making decisions about their illustrations and the words they will use to label them. After each group presents and explains a labeled illustration to the entire class, the illustrations are displayed on a bulletin board. Next the children identify three areas of the school grounds where they can examine litter in their school environment.

CA CCSS for ELA/Literacy: RL.K.1; RF.K.2; W.K.2; SL.K.1, 6; L.K.6

CA ELD Standards: ELD.PI.K.1–2, 5, 6, 9–11, 12b; ELD.K.PII.1, 3

The snapshots and vignettes cited above can be found in their entirety at https://www.cde.ca.gov/ci/rl/cf/, *2014 English Language Arts/English Language Development Framework*, p. 219.

Notes

The California ELD
Standards Companion

The California ELD Standards Companion

Grades K–2

Ivannia Soto and Linda Carstens

with Jim Burke

Foreword by Laurie Olsen

CORWIN

FOR INFORMATION:

Corwin
A SAGE Company
2455 Teller Road
Thousand Oaks, California 91320
(800) 233-9936
www.corwin.com

SAGE Publications Ltd.
1 Oliver's Yard
55 City Road
London EC1Y 1SP
United Kingdom

SAGE Publications India Pvt. Ltd.
B 1/I 1 Mohan Cooperative Industrial Area
Mathura Road, New Delhi 110 044
India

SAGE Publications Asia-Pacific Pte. Ltd.
18 Cross Street #10-10/11/12
China Square Central
Singapore 048423

Program Director and Publisher: Dan Alpert
Content Development Editor: Lucas Schleicher
Senior Editorial Assistant: Mia Rodriguez
Production Editor: Tori Mirsadjadi
Copy Editor: Diane DiMura
Typesetter: C&M Digitals (P) Ltd.
Proofreader: Victoria Reed-Castro
Cover and Interior Designer: Gail Buschman
Marketing Manager: Maura Sullivan

Library of Congress Cataloging-in-Publication Data

Names: Soto, Ivannia, author. | Carstens, Linda, author. | Burke, Jim, 1961- author.

Title: The California ELD standards companion. Grades K-2 / Ivannia M. Soto and Linda Carstens, with Jim Burke.

Description: Thousand Oaks, California : Corwin, 2019. | Includes index.

Identifiers: LCCN 2018030823 | ISBN 9781544301235 (spiral : alk. paper)

Subjects: LCSH: English language—Study and teaching—Foreign speakers—Standards—California. | English language—Study and teaching (Elementary)—Standards—California. | Language arts—Correlation with content subjects—California. | Limited English-proficient students—California.

Classification: LCC PE1128.A2 S59499 2019 | DDC 372.652/109794—dc23
LC record available at https://lccn.loc.gov/2018030823

This book is printed on acid-free paper.

SUSTAINABLE FORESTRY INITIATIVE
Certified Chain of Custody
Promoting Sustainable Forestry
www.sfiprogram.org
SFI-01268
SFI label applies to text stock

18 19 20 21 22 10 9 8 7 6 5 4 3 2 1

Contents

Foreword

Students enroll in California schools speaking languages representing every corner of the globe. Immigrant and U.S.-born, they collectively speak over 100 languages—and 1.2 million of them don't yet have the English skills needed to adequately comprehend, participate in, and access the educational program without support. The United States has always been a multilingual nation, but the challenge of educating a multilingual student population in an era of high academic standards is a 21st century challenge—shaped significantly by 20th century battles.

Ever since the 1974 Supreme Court ruled in the *Lau v. Nichols* case that the English language barrier was an impediment to equal education opportunity for students who do not speak English, schools have been charged with taking affirmative steps to provide access to the curriculum in comprehensible ways while teaching English to levels of proficiency needed for meaningful participation in an academic program. Easier said than done!

The journey of educators began back then, almost a half century ago, to figure out how to teach English effectively and sufficiently for rigorous academic work, and how to scaffold English Language Learners' comprehension and participation while they are learning English. In a nation in which language is always political, and the education of English Language Learners always at the cross-hairs of larger social battles, the journey has had significant turns and twists. The full meaning of familiarizing teachers with new English Language Development (ELD) standards in our current era and equipping them to actually use the standards as a tool to guide instruction can only be understood in the context of what has gone before.

Landmark civil rights legislation in the 1960s named national origin as one of the classes of people for whom equal protection under the law and whose rights to equal educational opportunity addressed. The *Lau* decision was the clarifying legal framework setting in motion the scramble by educators to figure out how to do it. And while it did not describe HOW to teach English and provide access, the *Castañeda* court decision one decade later laid out guidance for educators: Whatever is done must be based upon sound educational theory and/or research, it must be implemented with sufficient resources for that theory to actually work, and you must be able to show results over a period of time. There was no educational theory or research yet at the time. Though there was experience with English as a Second Language since World War I in the context of the military's work with adults— it had not been developed or tested for use with children or for application to academic settings. The need for sound theory and research was clear.

California actually took the lead by pulling together key theorists who might have parts of the answer for how to teach English Language Learners. Linguists, developmental psychologists, researchers working in other nations with immigrant and bilingual education were approached by the California Department of Education—and a remarkable group answered the call. Names still read in teacher preparation courses (people like Jim Cummins, Eleanor Thonis, Stephen Krashen, Tracy Terrell, and others) worked to put together a Theoretical Framework for Language Minority Students providing educators with key concepts like comprehensible input, the difference between first- and second-language development, language acquisition, the distinction between basic social language

(Basic Interpersonal Communicative Speech) and the language of books and academic study (Cognitive Academic Language Proficiency), the natural approach, communicative competency, the dual language brain, transfer, for example. And educators worked to pilot and refine the application of those concepts in classrooms with English Language Learners. Throughout the 1970s and 1980s all of this application occurred in the context of bilingual programs where the teaching and development of English was part and parcel of the use of bilingual approaches to enhance comprehensibility and access and to support overall language development through transfer and cross-linguistic relationships. Until increasing immigration and refugee resettlement combined with an economic recession gave opening to an English Only movement and backlash against bilingual approaches. English Language Development—the ENGLISH part of the equation—was expected to stand alone.

By the time No Child Left Behind (NCLB) was instituted with its powerful accountability hammers and a laser-like beam on closing achievement gaps for subgroups—including English Language Learners—English Language Development was fingered in California as the primary approach and support for serving English Learners. But ELD was caught in reading wars and prescriptive one-size-fits-all materials where ELD was conflated by many with reading interventions. It was a time of a narrow vision of language, reducing it largely to a focus on reading and reducing reading to a focus on foundational reading skills. As the National Literacy Panel on Language Minority Children and Youth reported, English Language Learners need those foundational reading skills, but they are not sufficient to address the language needs of a second-language learner. ELD instruction became further and further afield from a linguistic research base. Meanwhile, California state monitoring of services for English Language Learners repeatedly found that ELD was a major area of noncompliance. So teachers were feeling increasing pressure to deliver ELD, but not given appropriate or adequate materials, tools, and resources to do so. It was for many teachers of English Language Learners an era of discouragement, frustration, and confusion.

And then, along came the Common Core Language Arts Standards. In comparison to previous English Language Arts Standards, they were stunning in the degree to which they realigned with the research on language development, and the broader vision of language and its role in learning all other content areas was a welcome relief after the narrowness of the No Child Left Behind era. If English Language Development was going to be about supporting English Language Learners to develop the English needed for academic engagement in the Common Core era, clearly a revamp of the old ELD Standards was needed. By the time the new ELD Standards were released, followed by the historic combined ELA/ELD Framework, the new vision was clear. The shift from previous standards and practices was stunning. Rather than a focus on a narrow set of foundational reading skills and a lockstep progression of English skills, language development was now positioned as integrated in and across all academic content areas. Language is how those academic disciplines are learned, and the academic disciplines are the appropriate context in which to develop academic language. The integration of language and content opened the door for the kind of support and intentional language development English Language Learners need throughout their curriculum. *Integrated* and *Designated* ELD were added to the concept and terminology for how we understand ELD. Rather than follow a set scope and sequence along a set continuum toward proficiency, ELD was now to be responsive to student needs, designed in preparation for and response to the language demands of the academic work in which students are engaged. This is a powerful understanding and vision of language development—but it is far more nuanced and more difficult to plan and deliver than the old "follow the pacing plan in the teacher's guide" approach.

For teachers and administrators who had been schooled in, practiced in, and to some degree traumatized by the NCLB years, these new standards are a major shift and for many, a heavy lift. They not only need to come to grips with new standards, but also need to sort through and unlearn the discipline and beliefs about language and English Language Learners pounded into place during the No Child Left Behind era. Having followed orders and delivered the ELD they were supposed to do, but with inadequate tools and resources to do it, teachers often entered into becoming acquainted with the new ELD Standards not just as a set of standards to teach, but as a confusing subject carrying the baggage of discouraging experiences in trying to make it work in the past.

To pull off this new era of English Language Development, and to address the needs of our English Language Learners in an era of rigorous academic demands, it is essential that teachers be provided support and guidance in making meaning of the standards, understanding the shifts from previous practice, looking at the linguistic demands of academic tasks and content, and learning how to actually use the standards to plan instruction—in Designated ELD settings and in the context of Integrated ELD throughout the curriculum.

This is an era of extraordinary promise and support for addressing the needs of our English Language Learner students. In July of 2017, the California State Board of Education unanimously passed a new sweeping English Language Learner policy superseding the 1998 policy and leading our state into the 21st century. Hailed as "revolutionary," the new policy sets a comprehensive and aspirational vision for our state of schools that affirm, welcome, and respond to the needs of English Language Learners, preparing them with the linguistic, academic, and social skills needed for college, career, and civic participation in a global, diverse, and multilingual world. The policy centers on four research-based principles:

1. *Assets Oriented and Needs-Responsive* schools that value and build upon the cultural and linguistic assets students bring

2. A commitment to *Intellectual Quality of Instruction and Meaningful Access* through experiences that foster high levels of English proficiency, integrate language development and content learning, and provide for comprehension and participation through native language instruction and scaffolding

3. *Systems Conditions that Support Effectiveness* including building the capacity of educators to be knowledgeable of and able to leverage the strengths and meet the needs of English Language Learners

4. To ensure *Alignment and Articulation Within and Across Systems* beginning with a strong foundation in early childhood and continuing through to reclassification, graduation, and higher education.

This book, *The California ELD Standards Companion*, is a powerful tool for enacting the new visionary EL Roadmap policy. The work of this book is central to two of the principles. Principle #2, calling for meaningful access and intellectual quality of instruction, explicitly names ELD as a crucial element, reading as follows: *"language development occurs in and through content and is integrated across the curriculum, including integrated ELD and designated content-based ELD."* And Principle #3, seeking to build strong systems of support for English Language Learner services, explicitly calls for professional development and collaboration time for teachers to enable them to plan for responsive instruction.

That's why *The California ELD Standards Companion* is so important. It provides a step-by-step path for teachers to make meaning of how the set of ELD Standards are put together, dissect the standards, and then delve into what it actually looks like in instruction to address the standards. Teachers are provided definitions for key words and phrases that demystify the standards and provide support for reading the text of the ELD Standards, which are laden with linguistic terminology. And each section of the book includes a highly practical description of what teachers actually DO in the process of implementing standards-based ELD. This book is exactly the kind of bridge teachers need between standards and what it means for them in the classroom with their students. Concrete and practical, *The California ELD Standards Companion* guides teachers to be able to use the standards to forge a path that gives English Language Learners the power of language they need for educational participation, access, and success.

Laurie Olsen, PhD
Strategic Advisor to the Sobrato Early Academic Language (SEAL) Initiative
Sobrato Family Foundation

Prologue

To teachers of English learners (and we are *all* teachers of English learners)

At this point in history, we are well poised in California to ensure language equity on behalf of English Language Learners (ELLs). Key leverage points and systems—including the CA ELD Standards, ELA/ELD Framework, the English Language Proficiency Assessments for California (ELPAC), the EL Roadmap, and Proposition 58—make this a pivotal time for ELLs to make measurable academic progress, in the manner that they have always deserved.

Figure 1   Leverage Points for Language Literacy (Soto, 2017)

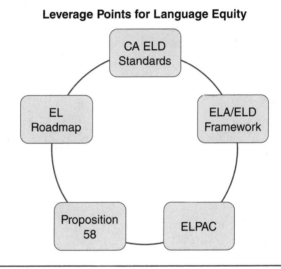

The CA ELD standards provide rigorous language expectations that our ELLs have needed to succeed in both language and across content areas. As educators, we have the gift of having the ELD standards align with the ELA standards, as well as the ELA/ELD Framework. We no longer need to learn a whole new set of standards that do not connect with our teaching throughout the school day. There is also no longer a disconnect between what is expected of native English speakers and ELLs. Instead, the two sets of standards— ELD and ELA—should work in tandem with each other. During Integrated ELD, content area standards are at the forefront, but we use the ELD standards to provide a *language scaffold* for that content. The focus, then, of Designated ELD should be language with the ELD standards at the forefront, but instruction should be *connected to content instruction*. That is, teachers are now free to do what we have known was best all along: connect language to content, so that language instruction is not disconnected from what happens throughout the rest of the school day.

Figure 2 ELD Working in Tandem (CDE, 2016)

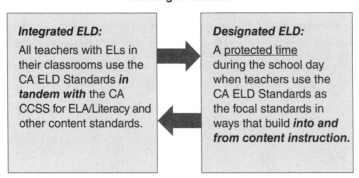

**Integrated and Designated ELD:
Working in Tandem**

> **Integrated ELD:**
> All teachers with ELs in their classrooms use the CA ELD Standards *in tandem with* the CA CCSS for ELA/Literacy and other content standards.

> **Designated ELD:**
> A protected time during the school day when teachers use the CA ELD Standards as the focal standards in ways that build *into and from content instruction.*

The ELA/ELD Framework provides both the research base and practical examples via snapshots (individual lessons) and vignettes (units of study) of both Integrated and Designated ELD in action, as well as across grade levels and content areas. We have included key snapshots and vignettes that correspond to the standards being addressed throughout this companion series. The framework can assist us with making sure that we are appropriately integrating and teaching to the rigorous expectations of the ELD Standards.

The English Learner Proficiency Assessments for California (ELPAC) is aligned with the ELD Standards, and assesses listening, speaking, reading, and writing. Instead of assessing language out of context, this rigorous language assessment is also contextualized and embedded in content. For example, ELLs are no longer expected to listen to and retell a story about chocolate chip cookies, but instead must actively listen to an academic presentation and paraphrase key content. This suggests that we must know and teach the ELD Standards deeply, in order for ELLs to be successful with this new assessment.

The California English Learner Roadmap State Board of Education Policy: Educational Programs and Services for English Learners was passed by the State Board of Education on July 12, 2017. This policy is intended to provide guidance to local educational agencies (LEAs) in order to welcome, understand, and educate the diverse population of students who are English learners attending California public schools (CDE, 2017). There are four principles, which undergird this new policy, which include the following:

- **Principle One:** Assets-Oriented and Needs Responsive Schools
- **Principle Two:** Intellectual Quality of Instruction and Meaningful Access
- **Principle Three:** System Conditions that Support Effectiveness
- **Principle Four:** Alignment and Articulation Within and Across Systems

The vision and mission of the EL Roadmap, according to the California Department of Education website, are as follows, and further provide direction for educational systems regarding *how* to create equitable educational environments for ELLs.

Vision

English Language Learners fully and meaningfully access and participate in a 21st century education from early childhood through Grade 12 that results in their attaining high levels of English proficiency, mastery of grade-level standards, and opportunities to develop proficiency in multiple languages.

Mission

California schools affirm, welcome, and respond to a diverse range of English Language Learner (ELL) strengths, needs, and identities. California schools prepare graduates with the linguistic, academic, and social skills and competencies they require for college, career, and civic participation in a global, diverse, and multilingual world, thus ensuring a thriving future for California (CDE, 2017).

Lastly, Proposition 58 does away with strict English only policies in California. In the fall of 2016, Proposition 58, the California state ballot that created more opportunities for bilingual education, passed with overwhelming public support, at 73.5 percent. The research base has proven that students who are able to speak, read, and write in two or more languages are able to participate in several different cultural and language worlds. Additionally, multilingual proficiency actually strengthens how the brain functions. Bilingualism is also associated with more cognitive flexibility and better problem solving abilities. Children who are bilingual tend to also perform better on achievement tests (Californians Together, 2017). Under Proposition 58, ELLs (and native English speakers) in California will once again be honored for their primary languages, and have an opportunity to become bilingual *and* biliterate. ELLs in bilingual programs in California are also required and expected to master the ELD and ELA standards. As such, they are also required to have participated in Designated and Integrated ELD, so all teachers must know these standards well in order for student mastery to occur.

It is an exciting time to be a teacher of ELLs in California! Understanding and teaching to the ELD Standards is one way to contribute to language equity. *The California ELD Standards Companion* should and can be used as a resource to assist educators in understanding the standards deeply so that they can better instruct and prepare ELLs around these more rigorous expectations. We recommend that teachers focus in and study the standards at their grade level, perhaps as a department or grade-level team. Then, they can use this resource to design their own lessons or units of study.

Preface

All too often, teachers who are trying to really make sense of the Common Core State Standards (CCSS) and the California English Language Development Standards will find themselves on a Sunday night with standards documents spread out all over their kitchen tables. *And these are no small documents!* They leave no room for that cup of tea (or glass of wine) on the surface to accompany lesson planning time.

As educators, we know that scaffolding is meant to be a support, to be used to build understanding and mastery. Scaffolding both the ELA and ELD standards documents is our intent with this *California ELD Standards Companion* series, so that teachers, coaches, and principals can go to one well-organized source for their needs. Over the years, we have heard these kinds of questions from teachers about the ELD Standards:

1. How do I know which ELA standards are correlated with a particular ELD Standard? The *California ELD Standards* document just cites numbers. Am I really working toward an ELA standard with my lesson?

2. What if I am trying to use the ELD Standards with other content areas, not just ELA? How do I know they will link to other content?

3. What are the important differences between the performance levels of an ELD Standard? What do these differences look like in teaching students at the three levels?

4. What do some of the terms mean in the Standards language? I don't have time (or space) to add a dictionary to the stuff already on my table.

It is with these questions in mind that we developed the format for the *California ELD Standards Companion* series. With some adaptations to the Corwin Common Core Companion books (linked to ELA), we have laid out these resources in one convenient place for each ELD Standard within the grade span:

- Charts with the correlated ELA standards in easy view, so no more digging across documents
- Examples of the ELD Standards used with other content areas, in both the What the Teacher Does and the Snapshots and Vignettes sections
- Definitions of terms used in the Standards, in kid-friendly language in the What the Student Does section, and in teacher terms with examples in the Academic Vocabulary section
- The three performance levels of the ELD Standard by grade level, with highlighting of the "build" between the Emerging, Expanding, and Bridging levels

It is our hope that this set of *California ELD Standards Companion* books, whether you are using the K–2, 3–5, 6–8, or 9–12 versions, will open up some space on your kitchen table and also clear up some space in your thinking to do successful lesson and unit planning for your ELL students. And maybe even for your cup of tea!

Acknowledgments

We would like to acknowledge the Whittier College students who worked alongside of Dr. Soto on this project: Adrianna Negus and Hollie Hollingsworth. You will both make fine teachers!

Publisher's Acknowledgments

Corwin gratefully acknowledges the contributions of the following reviewers:

Rebecca Castro
Elementary Principal
La Merced Elementary School
Montebello, CA

Michele R. Dean, Ed.D.
University Field Placement Coordinator & Lecturer
California Lutheran University
Thousand Oaks, CA

Mathew Espinosa
Coordinator, Multilingual Literacy
Sacramento City Unified School District
Sacramento, CA

Dr. Kathe Gonsalves
Coordinator, Language & Literacy Department
San Joaquin County Office of Education
Stockton, CA

Overall Introduction

Becoming Familiar With the California English Language Development (ELD) Standards—Like No Other

Whether educators and parents are already familiar with English Language Arts (ELA) standards from California or the Common Core State Standards, or know about ELD standards from other organizations (e.g., Texas, New York, WIDA)—a first look at the *California ELD Standards* (November 2012) will come as a surprise. Anyone looking for the traditional categories of Reading, Writing, Speaking, and Listening will come away scratching his or her head and saying, "*Where did they go? What are these things in place of the standards that I know?*"

Because the CA ELD Standards form the basis of the content for our *ELD Standards Companion*, it is a good idea to take a brief look at the organization of these standards, revised in November 2012. Here are the distinctive features in the organization of the CA ELD Standards:

- The ELD Standards are now organized into two main parts, each with three subcategories based on language function. The page following this introduction provides a summary of each of the main parts and subcategories. The traditional areas of Reading, Writing, Listening, and Speaking have been subsumed within areas of productive and receptive language, oral and written production, and comprehension.
- But that doesn't mean teachers can't find how the ELD Standards are related to the ELA standards. On each page of ELD Standards, there is a left-hand column titled "Texts and Discourse in Context," which lists the corresponding ELA standards for each ELD Standard.
- There are now three proficiency levels—Emerging, Expanding, and Bridging— instead of the five from earlier standards documents. The reduction from five to three offers a broader "catchment area" for describing student performance within the level. The highest level, Bridging, has been aligned with the California and Common Core State Standards in English Language Arts.

But Wait . . . There's More!

In addition to the ELD Standards themselves in grade spans K–12, the *California ELD Standards* document also contains several chapters related to the research and practice of teaching English Language Learners.

Chapter 4, "Theoretical Foundations and the Research Base of the California ELD Standards," provides research evidence and theory that was used in the development of the CA ELD Standards. These underpinnings ensure that the ELD Standards are aligned with current language and content learning research, and also that they provide commensurate expectations with ELA standards and content standards in other disciplines.

Chapter 5, "Learning About How English Works," provides a current base in supporting ELLs in understanding academic English and in using it proficiently.

Chapter 6, "Foundational Literacy Skills for English Learners," offers key findings regarding foundational literacy skills instruction for ELLs.

The **Glossary of Key Terms**, which is also available online, provides definitions and examples of key terms used in the CA ELD Standards.

Classroom Snapshots and Vignettes are also available online from www.cde.gov, highlighting classroom practices at various grade levels and subject areas related to each ELD Standard. These snapshots and vignettes have been summarized in this *ELD Standards Companion* for easy correlation to the specific standards for their use.

A Brief Orientation to *The California ELD Standards Companion*

Our *California ELD Standards Companion* takes the substance of the *California ELD Standards* document and rearranges it into manageable chunks for easy reference. For example, our organization highlights one ELD Standard at a time, building in the performance levels, links to ELA standards, key terms, and classroom snapshots and vignettes. Teachers will not have to flip pages and sections in order to see the related materials for a standard—they are all together and handy to use!

By design, our *ELD Standards Companion* has a number of features in common with Jim Burke's format in the *Common Core Companion* series, which focus on the Common Core English Language Arts standards. These complementary features make it possible for someone familiar with the *Common Core Companion* series to pick up the *ELD Standards Companion* and get right to work. These familiar features include

- *Clearly-organized standards and kid-friendly translation.* Each CA ELD Standard appears at the beginning of the section, incorporating the grade levels in the grade span (K–2, 3–5, 6–8, or 9–12) and the three performance levels of each standard (Emerging, Expanding, and Bridging). The same standard is "translated" into "kid-friendly" language (called the *Gist*) on the next page, so that teachers can see what students need to do in order to show mastery of the standard, again organized by grade level and performance level.
- *Incorporation of literature and information reading standards listed together, not separated out.* This design makes it easier to see how the standard builds across literary genres, performance levels, and grade levels.
- *Instructional techniques/What the teacher does.* In this section, there are specific suggestions for teaching related to the standard itself, providing an answer to the question, "*What would this look like in practice?*" For each standard, there is instructional differentiation provided by language performance level.
- *Academic vocabulary: key words and phrases.* Each standard is highlighted by a specific glossary of words, terms, and phrases that form part of the understanding of that standard. In many cases, there are examples of the word or term in use.

Equally important are the ways in which this ELD companion also has several unique features. These unique features include

- *Inclusion of the corresponding ELA Speaking and Listening and ELA Language standards.* Each CA ELD Standard is correlated with its Common Core ELA Speaking and Listening and Language standards so that the teacher has a sense of confidence that teaching ELD Standards is also working toward mastery of ELA standards. These correlations were developed by the writers of the *California ELD Standards* document itself.
- *Snapshots and vignettes.* The final section for each standard summarizes appropriate snapshots and vignettes of classroom practices that demonstrate progress toward the standard. These are classrooms with successful instruction designed for English Language Learners. Teachers are encouraged to read the entire snapshot or vignette on the California Department of Education website if they want more information.

All together, we hope that the familiar features and the new ones of both the *CA ELD Standards* and the *ELA Companion* add up to a valuable resource for teachers working with English Language Learners in classroom settings.

Part 1

INTERACTING IN MEANINGFUL WAYS

A Collaborative Mode

Introduction

Part I of the *California ELD Standards* promotes English Language Learners' abilities to *interact in meaningful ways* so that they acquire English and develop content knowledge simultaneously. Part I **comes first in the standards** to emphasize that students need to interact with adults and each other about meaning and content in order to build background knowledge and provide context before they enter deeply into how the English language works. Part I, Interacting in Meaningful Ways, is subdivided into three clusters of standards that emphasize student participation in the major modes of communication: Collaborative, Interpretive, and Productive.

Cluster A: Collaborative Mode Standards have the same general descriptions K–12 for the four standards in the cluster, related to engagement in dialogue with others. These include

1. *Exchanging information and ideas with others through oral collaborative conversations on a range of social and academic topics.* Teachers can structure collaborative learning practices for small-group discussion about the texts students read across subject areas. These practices help students learn the content, vocabulary, and grammatical structures related to the texts in language-rich, iterative social situations. While this standard can be applied to conversations around academic texts, it can also be applied to any type of conversation (social or academic) or to conversations that arise during collaborative group work (Heller & Greenleaf, 2007; Vaughn et al., 2011).

2. *Interacting with others in written English in various communicative forms (print, communicative technology, and multimedia).* This standard is specific to collaborating through written English (e.g., passing notes, written feedback, collaborative group writing/multimedia projects, collaboration using technology) but also includes word-level processing such as decoding and spelling. It also includes recognizing the organizational features of different academic texts so that students can better comprehend and create their own written texts (Brisk 2012; Gibbons, 2008; Hammond, 2006).

3. *Offering and supporting opinions and negotiating with others in communicative exchanges.* Not all students come to school knowing how to engage in collaborative discussions with others. Recent research has shown that ELLs can learn how to do this by being "apprenticed" through scaffolded interactions in classroom discussion settings (Gibbons, 2009; Walqui & van Lier, 2010).

4. *Adapting language choices to various contexts (based on task, purpose, audience, and text type).* Choosing the right language depends on what is happening (the content), who is communicating and their relationship (e.g., peer to peer, student to adult), how the message is conveyed (e.g., written, spoken), and whether the communication is formal or informal (Schleppegrell, 2012). Student success with adapting language choices grows with student ability to increase vocabulary, recognize and use appropriate register, use more complex sentence and clauses, and use connecting/transitioning words to convey meaning (O'Dowd, 2010; Schleppegrell, 2004).

In *The California ELD Companion*, the What the Student Does section provides specific descriptions of competence with each of the Collaborative standards at the appropriate grade range and proficiency level. Similarly, the What the Teacher Does section provides specific strategies for developing competence with each of the Collaborative standards at the appropriate grade range. And the last section, Vignettes and Snapshots, offers classroom-level descriptions of what each standard looks like in practice.

Source: *California English Language Development Standards, K–12* (2012). Chapter 4, "Theoretical Foundations and the Research Bases of the CA ELD Standards," provides an excellent summary of the research used in developing the four Collaborative standards in Part I, A.

Emerging

K Contribute to conversations and express ideas by asking and answering *yes-no* and *wh-* questions and responding using gestures, words, and simple phrases.

1 Contribute to conversations and express ideas by asking and answering *yes-no* and *wh-* questions and responding using gestures, words, and simple phrases.

2 Contribute to conversations and express ideas by asking and answering *yes-no* and *wh-* questions and responding using gestures, words, and learned phrases.

Expanding

K Contribute to *class, group, and partner discussions by listening attentively, following turn-taking rules*, and asking and answering questions.

1 Contribute to *class, group, and partner discussions by listening attentively, following turn-taking rules*, and asking and answering questions.

2 Contribute to *class, group, and* partner discussions, *including sustained dialogue, by listening attentively, following turn-taking rules, asking relevant questions, affirming others, and adding relevant information*.

Bridging

K Contribute to class, group, and partner discussions by listening attentively, following turn-taking rules, and asking and answering questions.

1 Contribute to class, group, and partner discussions by listening attentively, following turn-taking rules, and asking and answering questions.

2 Contribute to class, group, and partner discussions, including sustained dialogue, by listening attentively, following turn-taking rules, asking relevant questions, affirming others, adding pertinent information, *building on responses, and providing useful feedback*.

Script **in bold italics** indicates content not found in earlier proficiency levels of the same ELD Standard.

Source: *California English Language Development Standards for Grades K–12*, California Department of Education (November 2012).

Notes

What the **Student** Does

Emerging	Expanding	Bridging
Gist: *Students have conversations with others, follow norms for discussion, and stay on topic through multiple exchanges.*		
K They consider: • Do I contribute to the conversations and express my own ideas? • Do I ask and answer yes/no questions? Who, what, when, where, why questions? • Do I use gestures, words, and simple phrases to help others understand what I am saying?	**K** They *also* consider: • Do I take part in class, group, and partner discussions? • Do I listen attentively? • Do I follow turn-taking rules? • Do I ask and answer questions?	**K** Same as Expanding.
Gist: *Students have conversations with classmates and adults, follow norms for discussion, build on one another's ideas, and ask questions.*		
1 They consider: • Do I contribute to the conversations and express my own ideas? • Do I ask and answer yes/no questions? Who, what, when, where, why questions? • Do I use gestures, words, and simple phrases to help others understand what I am saying?	**1** They *also* consider: • Do I take part in class, group, and partner discussions? • Do I listen attentively? • Do I follow turn-taking rules? • Do I ask and answer questions?	**1** Same as Expanding.
Gist: *Students have conversations with classmates and adults in small and large groups, follow norms for discussion, build on one another's ideas by linking their comments, and ask questions for clarification and explanation.*		
2 They consider: • Do I contribute to the conversations and express my own ideas? • Do I ask and answer yes/no questions? Who, what, when, where, why questions? • Do I use gestures, words, and learned phrases to help others understand what I am saying?	**2** They *also* consider: • Do I take part in class, group, and partner discussions with multiple exchanges? • Do I listen attentively? • Do I follow turn-taking rules? • Do I ask relevant questions? • Do I take time to affirm others (say that I understand their point)? • Do I add relevant information?	**2** They *also* consider: • Do I help keep the discussion moving forward? • Do I add to other people's responses? • Do I let others know when their comments are helpful to me?

Source: *California English Language Development Standards for Grades K–12* (2012).

Speaking and Listening Standards	Language Standards
K SL.K.1: Participate in collaborative conversations with diverse partners about *kindergarten topics and texts* with peers and adults in small and larger groups. a. Follow agreed-upon rules for discussions (e.g., listening to others and taking turns speaking about the topics and texts under discussion). b. Continue a conversation through multiple exchanges.	**K L.K.1:** Demonstrate command of the conventions of standard English grammar and usage when writing or speaking. a. Print many upper- and lowercase letters. Use frequently occurring nouns and verbs. b. Form regular plural nouns orally by adding /s/ or /es/. c. Understand and use question words (interrogatives). d. Use the most frequently occurring prepositions (e.g., *to, from, in, out, on, off, for, of, by, with*). e. Produce and expand complete sentences in shared language activities.
K SL.K.6: Speak audibly and express thoughts, feelings, and ideas clearly.	**K L.K.6:** Use words and phrases acquired through conversations, reading and being read to, and responding to texts.
1 SL.1.1: Participate in collaborative conversations with diverse partners about *grade 1 topics and texts* with peers and adults in small and larger groups. a. Follow agreed-upon rules for discussions (e.g., listening to others with care, speaking one at a time about the topics and texts under discussion). b. Build on others' talk in conversations by responding to the comments of others through multiple exchanges. c. Ask questions to clear up any confusion about the topics and texts under discussion.	**1 L.1.1:** Demonstrate command of the conventions of standard English grammar and usage when writing or speaking. a. Print all upper- and lowercase letters. b. Use common, proper, and possessive nouns. c. Use singular and plural nouns with matching verbs in basic sentences (e.g., *He hops; We hop*). d. Use personal, possessive, and indefinite pronouns. e. Use verbs to convey a sense of past, present, and future. f. Use frequently occurring adjectives. g. Use frequently occurring conjunctions (e.g., *and, but, or so, because*). h. Use determiners (e.g., articles, demonstratives). i. Use frequently occurring prepositions (e.g., *during, beyond, toward*). j. Produce and expand complete simple and compound declarative, interrogative, imperative, and exclamatory sentences in response to prompts.

continued

continued from previous

Speaking and Listening Standards	Language Standards
1 **SL.1.6:** Produce complete sentences when appropriate to task and situation. (See grade 1 Language standards 1 and 3 for specific expectations)	**1** **L.1.6:** Use words and phrases acquired through conversations, reading and being read to, and responding to texts, including using frequently occurring conjunctions to signal simple relationships (e.g., *because*).
2 **SL.2.1:** Participate in collaborative conversations with diverse partners about *grade 2 topics and texts* with peers and adults in small and larger groups. a. Follow agreed-upon rules for discussions (e.g., gaining the floor in respectful ways, listening to others with care, speaking one at a time about the topics and texts under discussion). b. Build on others' talk in conversations by linking their comments to the remarks of others. c. Ask for clarification and further explanation as needed about the topics and texts under discussion.	**2** **L.2.1:** Demonstrate command of the conventions of standard English grammar and usage when writing or speaking. a. Use collective nouns (e.g., *group*). b. Form and use frequently occurring irregular plural nouns (e.g., *feet, children, teeth, mice, fish*). c. Use reflexive pronouns (e.g., *myself, ourselves*). d. Form and use the past tense of frequently occurring irregular verbs (e.g., *sat, hid, told*). e. Use adjectives and adverbs and choose between them depending on what is to be modified. f. Produce, expand, and rearrange complete simple and compound sentences (e.g., *The boy watched the movie; The little boy watched the movie; The action movie was watched by the little boy*).
	2 **L.2.3:** Use knowledge of language and its conventions when writing, speaking, reading, or listening. a. Compare formal and informal uses of English.
2 **SL.2.6:** Produce complete sentences when appropriate to task and situation in order to provide requested detail or clarification. (See grade 2 Language standards 1 and 3 for specific expectations)	**2** **L.2.6:** Use words and phrases acquired through conversations, reading and being read to, and responding to texts, including using adjectives and adverbs to describe (e.g., *When other kids are happy, that makes me happy*).

Source: *Common Core State Standards, K–12 English Language Arts* (2010).

What the **Teacher** Does

During the year, children engage daily in multiple discussions. Discussions occur in pairs, small groups, and with the entire class. Some discussions are adult led. Others are conducted by the children, with teacher guidance and monitoring. Teachers use a variety of structures for discussions and make sure that all children have ample opportunities to contribute, not just the most outspoken children. Furthermore, they ensure that children engage in discussions with diverse partners. That is, children do not always turn to the same one or two neighbors to respond to a prompt or share their thinking.

- **To teach students to contribute to discussions and express ideas:** Teach and demonstrate discussion behaviors that indicate respect for others, such as listening closely, not interrupting, responding to comments, encouraging others to contribute, and acknowledging and appreciating all participants' thinking on the topic.

- **To support students in asking and answering questions:** Use sentence frames with question prompts to demonstrate for students how to ask and answer questions at a variety of depth of knowledge levels. For example, *"How was this similar to . . . ?"* or *"What would happen if . . . ?"* or *"Can you defend your position about . . . ?"*

- **To help students to follow turn-taking:** Use role cards for listening and speaking to teach students how to take turns. For example, a role card with an ear for listening can be created on one side with language frames for listening, such as *"My partner said . . . ,"* can be used. Similarly, a speaking card with a mouth icon printed on one side with a language frame, such as *"I think . . ."* or *"I believe . . . ,"* can be used. In K–2, these role cards can be color coded with speaking in green for go and speak, and red for listening for stop and listen.

- **To demonstrate useful feedback for students:** Engage the children in reflection on the discussion process, such as asking them to consider what was helpful in keeping a discussion on target and what might have made the discussion run more smoothly.

Tips for Differentiation by Proficiency Level

- *Emerging*—Small groups are given images of resources that accompany the day's lesson and are prompted to draw on the images to capture what they learned during the lesson. Use basic sentence frames such as *"I think . . ."* or *"I see. . . ."*

- *Expanding*—Students may respond to sentence frames about the images, such as *"This image shows . . . ,"* *"This image is important because . . . ,"* or *"This image is related . . ."*

- *Bridging*—Students may study images, including photographs and illustrations, and then discuss in small groups or pairs with questions or sentence prompts to guide them.

Note: A variety of sentence frames should be used throughout the school year (notice the variety provided above). ELLs at the Emerging level will need the support of basic frames, but these frames should then be varied according to language purpose throughout the school year. ELLs at the bridging level should then be expected to use more sophisticated sentence frames or to have internalized the language, so that they no longer need them at all. Sentence frames should be used as a scaffold and not a crutch.

Source: 2014 *English Language Arts/English Language Development Framework*, p. 210; video links can be found at https://www.cde.ca.gov/ci/rl/cf/ implementationsupport.asp.

Academic Vocabulary—Key Words and Phrases Related to Standard 1: Exchanging information and ideas

Affirming others: Teacher or student comments that reflect a positive behavior (i.e., turn-taking) or a response or question from someone else in the conversation that exemplifies or clarifies the gist of the discussion.

Asking relevant questions or adding pertinent information: Teacher or student questions and/or comments that move forward the group's understanding of the concepts being studied. These are usually open ended, and can be text dependent, clarifying, and/or making connections questions or comments (to oneself or others, to other texts, to other ideas).

Building on other's responses: Student comments that take into account what others have said in the discussion, and linking their comments to those points.

Collaborative Conversations: Discussing ideas and working jointly with others to develop new thinking.

Multiple exchanges: Discussions where one idea is considered and discussed by several persons, growing richer and more complex as new ideas or examples are added, instead of the typical question/answer, new question/answer pattern that limits discussion.

Providing useful feedback: Offering specific, helpful suggestions to a student in order to improve his or her thinking or work product. Examples include *"You did a good job on _____"* or *"I think you should _____ because it would help _____."*

Speaking audibly: To speak loudly enough to be heard but not so loudly as to be shouting or distorting the message.

Sustained dialogue: Collaborative conversations in which students create new thinking by working with others to add details or further develop thoughts on the topic of discussion.

Turn-taking roles: Various ways for students to consciously listen to others, say their contribution, and then listen again. These roles can include Think-Pair-Share, Reciprocal Teaching, using Equity sticks, etc.

Using learned phrases: Opportunities for students to share their ideas and thoughts by using patterns or prompts to frame their oral language. These can come from pattern drills, sentence frames, and other sources.

Source: Taberski & Burke, (2014), *The Common Core Companion: The Standards Decoded, Grades K–2.*

Notes

Example of Practice in Snapshot Related to Standard 1: Exchanging information and ideas

Snapshot 3.4. Collecting and Reporting Data on Litter at School Integrated ELA, ELD, Science, and History–Social Science in Kindergarten

The kindergarteners in Mr. Kravitz's classroom listen to several informational and literary texts about the importance of caring for the environment and the impact litter has on local habitats. Mr. Kravitz guides a discussion about this type of pollution, asking—and encouraging the children to ask—questions about the information they are learning from the texts. He prepares them for paired as well as large-group conversations about what they are learning by revisiting the texts and images and drawing attention to some of the vocabulary that may be particularly useful for their discussions. For example, he reviews and writes on a chart some of the general academic (e.g., *discard, accumulate, observe, impact*) and domain-specific (e.g., *habitat, pollute, litter*) vocabulary from the texts that convey important ideas.

Next he has students meet in pairs to talk about what they have learned. Many of them refer to the chart to remind themselves and each other about the concepts and accompanying vocabulary. After sharing in pairs, the children gather in small groups to draw and label illustrations about what they learned and discussed. They work collaboratively, talking about their understandings and making decisions about their illustrations and the words they will use to label them. After each group presents and explains a labeled illustration to the entire class, the illustrations are displayed on a bulletin board. Next the children identify three areas of the school grounds where they can examine litter in their school environment.

CA CCSS for ELA/Literacy: RL.K.1; RF.K.2; W.K.2; SL.K.1, 6; L.K.6

CA ELD Standards: ELD.PI.K.1–2, 5, 6, 9–11, 12b; ELD.K.PII.1, 3

The snapshots and vignettes cited above can be found in their entirety at https://www.cde.ca.gov/ci/rl/cf/, 2014 *English Language Arts/English Language Development Framework*, p. 219.

Notes

Notes

Emerging

K Collaborate with the teacher and peers on joint composing projects of short informational and literary texts that include minimal writing (labeling with a few words), using technology, where appropriate, for publishing, graphics, and the like.

1 Collaborate with teacher and peers on joint writing projects of short informational and literary texts, using technology where appropriate for publishing, graphics, and the like.

2 Collaborate with peers on joint writing projects of short informational and literary texts, using technology where appropriate for publishing, graphics, and the like.

Expanding

K Collaborate with the teacher and peers on joint composing projects of informational and literary texts that include *some writing (e.g., short sentences)*, using technology, where appropriate, for publishing, graphics, and the like.

1 Collaborate with peers on joint writing projects of *longer informational and literary texts*, using technology where appropriate for publishing, graphics, and the like.

2 Collaborate with peers on joint writing projects of *longer informational and literary* texts, using technology where appropriate for publishing, graphics, and the like.

Bridging

K Collaborate with the teacher and peers on joint composing projects of informational and literary texts that include a *greater amount of writing (e.g., a very short story)*, using technology, where appropriate, for publishing, graphics, and the like.

1 Collaborate with peers on joint writing projects of longer informational and literary texts, using technology where appropriate for publishing, graphics, and the like.

2 Collaborate with peers on joint writing projects of a *variety of longer informational and literary* texts, using technology where appropriate for publishing, graphics, and the like.

Script **in bold italics** indicates content not found in earlier proficiency levels of the same ELD Standard.

Source: *California English Language Development Standards for Grades K–12*, California Department of Education (2012).

Notes

What the **Student** Does

Emerging	**Expanding**	**Bridging**

Gist: *With guidance and support from adults, students collaborate on joint composing projects ranging from minimal writing to short stories, using technology as appropriate.*

K They consider:	**K** They *also* consider:	**K** Same as Expanding.
• Do my classmates and I have a general idea of what we will write (purpose)? • Who will be the audience? Who will read it? • How can my classmates and I use this tool to write together?	• How can this tool make finding and organizing information and stories easier? • How can this tool help us publish and present writing?	

Gist: *With guidance and support from adults, students collaborate on joint composing projects ranging from shorter to longer texts, using technology as appropriate.*

1 They consider:	**1** They *also* consider:	**1** Same as Expanding.
• What is our joint purpose for writing? • Who will be the audience? Who will read it? • How can my classmates and I use this tool to write together?	• How can this tool make finding and organizing information and stories easier? • How can this tool help us publish and present writing?	

Gist: *With guidance and support from adults, students collaborate on joint composing projects ranging from shorter to longer texts, using technology as appropriate.*

2 They consider:	**2** They *also* consider:	**2** They *also* consider:
• What is our joint purpose for writing? • Who will be the audience? Who will read it? • How can my classmates and I use this tool to write together?	• How can this tool make finding and organizing information and stories easier? • How can this tool help us publish and present writing?	• How will our use of technology help share our joint message (i.e., publishing and graphics)?

Source: California English Language Development Standards for Grades K–12 (2012).

Speaking and Listening Standards	Language Standards
	K **L.K.1:** Demonstrate command of the conventions of standard English grammar and usage when writing or speaking. a. Print many upper- and lowercase letters. b. Use frequently occurring nouns and verbs. c. Form regular plural nouns orally by adding /s/ or /es/ (e.g., *dog, dogs; wish, wishes*). d. Understand and use question words (interrogatives) (e.g., *who, what, where, when, why, how*). e. Use the most frequently occurring prepositions (e.g., *to, from, in, out, on, off, for, of, by, with*). f. Produce and expand complete sentences in shared language activities.
	K **L.K.6:** Use words and phrases acquired through conversations, reading and being read to, and responding to texts.
	1 **L.1.1:** Demonstrate command of the conventions of standard English grammar and usage when writing or speaking. a. Print all upper- and lowercase letters. b. Use common, proper, and possessive nouns. c. Use singular and plural nouns with matching verbs in basic sentences (e.g., *He hops; We hop*). d. Use personal (subject, object), possessive, and indefinite pronouns (e.g., *I, me, my; they, them, their; anyone, everything*). e. Use verbs to convey a sense of past, present, and future (e.g., *Yesterday I walked home; Today I walk home; Tomorrow I will walk home*). f. Use frequently occurring adjectives. g. Use frequently occurring conjunctions (e.g., *and, but, or, so, because*). h. Use determiners (e.g., articles, demonstratives). i. Use frequently occurring prepositions (e.g., *during, beyond, toward*). j. Produce and expand complete simple and compound declarative, interrogative, imperative, and exclamatory sentences in response to prompts.

continued

continued from previous

Speaking and Listening Standards	Language Standards
	1 **L.1.6:** Use words and phrases acquired through conversations, reading and being read to, and responding to texts, including using frequently occurring conjunctions to signal simple relationships (e.g., *because*).
	2 **L.2.1:** Demonstrate command of the conventions of standard English grammar and usage when writing or speaking. a. Use collective nouns (e.g., *group*). b. Form and use frequently occurring irregular plural nouns (e.g., *feet, children, teeth, mice, fish*). c. Use reflexive pronouns (e.g., *myself, ourselves*). d. Form and use the past tense of frequently occurring irregular verbs (e.g., *sat, hid, told*). e. Use adjectives and adverbs, and choose between them depending on what is to be modified. f. Produce, expand, and rearrange complete simple and compound sentences (e.g., *The boy watched the movie; The little boy watched the movie; The action movie was watched by the little boy*). g. Create readable documents with legible print.
	2 **L.2.3:** Use knowledge of language and its conventions when writing, speaking, reading, or listening. a. Compare formal and informal uses of English.
	2 **L.2.6:** Use words and phrases acquired through conversations, reading and being read to, and responding to texts, including using adjectives and adverbs to describe (e.g., *When other kids are happy, that makes me happy*).

*In addition to the ELA Language standards provided in this chart, ELD Standard 2: Interacting via written English is **also** correlated with ELA Writing standards K.6, 1.6, and 2.6.*

Source: *Common Core State Standards, K–12 English Language Arts* (2010).

What the **Teacher** Does

A great deal of writing in kindergarten occurs when children—as an entire class, in small groups, or as individuals—dictate their ideas to an adult who records them. Children also express themselves in writing independently, beginning with marks and scribbles that soon become strings of letters. Eventually, as they learn about the sound structure of language (that is, they become phonemically aware) and about the symbols that represent sounds (that is, the letters of the alphabet), children begin to use that knowledge in their writing. Words are phonetically spelled at this stage of learning. This is an important milestone representing children's growing understanding of the alphabetic principle—crucial for independence in both writing and reading (*2014 ELA/ELD Framework*, p. 207).

Teachers and students can jointly compose projects of short informational and literary texts that include minimal writing (labeling with a few words):

- Teachers can chart student responses to picture prompts or instructional read alouds, in order to model the writing process.

- The teacher can model how to use a word bank to complete cloze passages that models effective writing.

Children progress considerably in their writing, both in terms of substance (including organization and style) and mechanics during Grade 1. They have daily opportunities to write with their teacher, their peers, and on their own for a variety of purposes and in a variety of contexts. They write in learning and literature response journals. They write messages to others. They write directions for visitors. They write lists of ways to improve the playground. Children learn to reflect on the effectiveness of their own and others' writing as they share their written work. Some selections are revised after feedback from the teacher or peers (W.1.5). Some are published, such as when each child contributes a page produced digitally to a class book. Children engage deeply with a number of texts, use language to communicate with peers, and problem solve as they pursue research topics and present in writing what they learned (W.1.7) (2014 ELA/ELD Framework, p. 242).

Teachers and students can jointly write projects of short informational and literary texts, using technology where appropriate for publishing, graphics, and the like:

- The teacher can continue to chart student responses to writing, as well as use sentence frames with word banks to complete their writing assignments.

- Teachers can provide contextualized ensure classroom experiences, such as exploring their playground or school garden, to build background knowledge and ensure that students have enough information to write about.

- Teachers can use a document camera to think aloud regarding writing prompts and model writing in a notebook or digital book.

- Teachers continue to read a variety of texts with students, in order to build background knowledge on topics being written about.

- The teacher can use graphic organizers with cloze passages that include language features such as transition words. For example, "*In the beginning of the story,* _____. *Secondly,* _____. *Lastly,* _____." The teacher can model for students how to complete their first response using details from a text. In pairs, students can complete the second sentence, and then each student can complete the last part.

- Using keyboarding skills in Grade 3 to produce and publish writing (W.2–3.6).

- The teacher can directly teach keyboarding skills and provide ample time for practice of such skills to produce writing.

Tips for Differentiation by Proficiency Level

- *Emerging*—Students at this proficiency level will need multiple scaffolds for the writing process, including collaborative and joint writing. Teachers can use picture prompts with word banks and chart student responses to model the writing process.

- *Expanding*—Cloze passages can be used, alongside of word banks, that teachers can chart student responses on.

- *Bridging*—Students can work collaboratively with each other, using cloze passage templates (or teacher charting), in order to compose joint writing selections. The teacher can ask students to discuss and then outline their thinking together, before completing assigned to certain sections.

Source: Taberski & Burke, (2014), *The Common Core Companion: The Standards Decoded, Grades K–2.*

Academic Vocabulary—Key Words and Phrases Related to Standard 2: Interacting via written English

Cloze passages: The strategy of deleting key words from within a written sentence or passage in order for the reader to determine the words from context and/or word banks.

Collaboration in writing: When students work together to generate ideas, conduct writing projects together, and respond to each other's writing projects (e.g., peer review and editing).

Publishing: Using computers and printers to publish their writing projects for classroom, school, and/or wider use online.

Sentence frames: If students are struggling to find the right words to explain, describe, and clarify what they are thinking, a sentence starter or sentence frame helps them to get the idea started. For example, *"I think the statement is true because _____"* or *"This makes me wonder _____."* Sentence frames can be either open ended or closed.

Technology: Using computers and tablets to compose, revise, and edit writing. It may also include using applications for finding information and creating graphics.

Writing mechanics: These are the conventions of print that do not exist in oral language, such as spelling, punctuation, capitalization, and paragraphs.

Writing projects: These may include traditional informational and literary pieces, but may also include technological writing forms (e.g., blogs, wikis, websites, and multimedia presentations).

Source: Taberski & Burke, (2014), *The Common Core Companion: The Standards Decoded, Grades K–2.*

Notes

Example of Practice in Snapshot Related to Standard 2: Interacting via written English

Vignette 3.1. Retelling and Rewriting *The Three Little Pigs* Integrated ELA/Literacy and ELD Instruction in Transitional Kindergarten

Ms. Campbell calls her students to the carpet and reminds them that they have been reading lots of different versions of *The Three Little Pigs*. She recalls that yesterday, they spent a lot of time retelling the story to one another and explains that today, they are going to use all of that great oral retelling to rewrite the story together. Using her computer tablet and a projector, Ms. Campbell projects five pictures depicting important events from the story. She asks her students to take turns with a partner retelling the story, using the pictures. She listens to the children as they share, noting the language they use, their ability to sequence events, and any misunderstandings.

Ms. Campbell [then] uses her computer tablet to project the Story Rewriting Template the class will use. The template uses the same terms as the story map and organizes the story grammar and sequence into three stages: *orientation*, *complication*, and *resolution*. Rather than using the terms *beginning*, *middle*, and *end* (which all text types have), Ms. Campbell finds that using the terms *orientation*, *complication*, and *resolution* helps students discuss story organization because the terms are related to what is happening at each stage of the narrative. She uses the template to guide students as they jointly reconstruct the story aloud. In the Story Rewriting Template, the template Ms. Campbell uses with students is on the left while her notes to herself about the function of each stage are on the right.

CA CCSS for ELA/Literacy: RL.K.1–3; W.K.3; SL.K.1–2; L.K.6
CA ELD Standards: ELD.PI.K.12a; ELD.PII.K.1, 2, 3b

The snapshots and vignettes cited above can be found in their entirety at https://www.cde.ca.gov/ci/rl/cf/, *2014 ELA/ELD Framework*, p. 186.

Notes

Notes

Emerging

K Offer opinions and ideas in conversations using a small set of learned phrases (e.g., *I think X*), as well as open responses.

1 Offer opinions and ideas in conversations using a small set of learned phrases (e.g., *I think X*), as well as open responses in order to gain and/or hold the floor.

2 Offer opinions and negotiate with others in conversations using learned phrases (e.g., *I think* X.), as well as open responses, in order to gain and/or hold the floor.

Expanding

K Offer opinions in conversations using an ***expanded set of learned phrases*** (e.g., I think/***don't think X. I agree with X***), as well as open responses, ***in order to gain and/or hold the floor***.

1 Offer opinions ***and negotiate with others*** in conversations using an ***expanded set of learned phrases*** (e.g., I think/***don't think X. I agree with X***), as well as open responses in order to gain and/or hold the floor, ***elaborate on an idea, and so on***.

2 Offer opinions and negotiate with others in conversations using an ***expanded set of learned phrases (e.g., I agree with X, but X.***), as well as open responses, in order to gain and/or hold the floor, ***provide counterarguments, and the like***.

Bridging

K Offer opinions in conversations using an expanded set of learned phrases (e.g., I *think/don't think X. I agree with X, but . . .*), as well as open responses, in order to gain and/or hold the floor ***or add information to an idea***.

1 Offer opinions and negotiate with others in conversations using an expanded set of learned phrases (e.g., I *think/don't think X. I agree with X*), and open responses in order to gain and/or hold the floor, elaborate on an idea, ***provide different opinions***, and so on.

2 Offer opinions and negotiate with others in conversations using a ***variety of learned phrases (e.g., That's a good idea, but X***), as well as open responses, in order to gain and/or hold the floor, provide counterarguments, ***elaborate on an idea***, and the like.

Script ***in bold italics*** indicates content not found in earlier proficiency levels of the same ELD Standard.

Source: *California English Language Development Standards for Grades K–12*, California Department of Education (November 2012).

Notes

What the **Student** Does

Emerging	Expanding	Bridging

Gist: Students offer their opinions and ideas in conversation using learned phrases, as well as open responses.

K They consider:

- Do I know how to start my opinion or idea using learned phrases?
- Do I know how to start my opinion or idea using open responses?

K They *also* consider:

- Is my opinion or idea related to what the rest of the class is talking about?
- Do I know how to gain and/or hold the floor during this conversation so that I can speak?

K They *also* consider:

- Do I help the conversation grow bigger by adding my opinion or idea?

Gist: Students offer their opinions and negotiate with others in conversations using an expanded set of learned phrases, as well as open responses, in order to gain or hold the floor, add to ideas, etc.

1 They consider:

- Do I know how to start my opinion or idea using learned phrases?
- Do I know how to start my opinion or idea using open responses?
- Do I know how to gain and/or hold the floor during this conversation so that I can speak?

1 They *also* consider:

- Can I negotiate with others in conversations?
- Do I listen carefully to my classmates when they speak so I can stay on topic?
- Do I help the conversation grow bigger by adding my opinion?

1 They *also* consider:

- Do I ask questions when I'm confused?
- Will my opinion add something new to the conversation?

Gist: Students offer their opinions and negotiate with others in conversations using an expanded set of learned phrases, as well as open responses, in order to gain or hold the floor, provide counterarguments, etc.

2 They consider:

- Do I know how to start my opinion or idea using learned phrases or open responses?
- Do I know how to gain and/or hold the floor during this conversation so that I can speak?
- Can I negotiate with others in conversations?

2 They *also* consider:

- Will my opinion offer a different argument to the conversation?

2 They *also* consider:

- Will my opinion add something new to the conversation?

Source: *California English Language Development Standards for Grades K–12 (2012).*

Speaking and Listening Standards	Language Standards
K **SL.K.1:** Participate in collaborative conversations with diverse partners about kindergarten topics and texts with peers and adults in small and larger groups. a. Follow agreed-upon rules for discussions (e.g., listening to others and taking turns speaking about the topics and texts under discussion). b. Continue a conversation through multiple exchanges.	**K** **L.K.1:** Demonstrate command of the conventions of standard English grammar and usage when writing or speaking. a. Print many upper- and lowercase letters. b. Use frequently occurring nouns and verbs. c. Form regular plural nouns orally by adding /s/ or /es/ (e.g., *dog, dogs; wish, wishes*). d. Understand and use question words (interrogatives) (e.g., *who, what, where, when, why, how*). e. Use the most frequently occurring prepositions (e.g., *to, from, in, out, on, off, for, of, by, with*). f. Produce and expand complete sentences in shared language activities.
K **SL.K.6:** Speak audibly and express thoughts, feelings, and ideas clearly.	**K** **L.K.6:** Use words and phrases acquired through conversations, reading and being read to, and responding to texts.
1 **SL.1.1:** Participate in collaborative conversations with diverse partners about grade 1 topics and texts with peers and adults in small and larger groups. a. Follow agreed-upon rules for discussions (e.g., listening to others with care, speaking one at a time about the topics and texts under discussion). b. Build on others' talk in conversations by responding to the comments of others through multiple exchanges. c. Ask questions to clear up any confusion about the topics and texts under discussion.	**1** **L.1.1:** Demonstrate command of the conventions of standard English grammar and usage when writing or speaking. a. Print all upper- and lowercase letters. b. Use common, proper, and possessive nouns. c. Use singular and plural nouns with matching verbs in basic sentences (e.g., *He hops; We hop*). d. Use personal (subject, object), possessive, and indefinite pronouns (e.g., *I, me, my; they, them, their; anyone, everything*). e. Use verbs to convey a sense of past, present, and future (e.g., *Yesterday I walked home; Today I walk home; Tomorrow I will walk home*). f. Use frequently occurring adjectives. g. Use frequently occurring conjunctions (e.g., *and, but, or, so, because*). h. Use determiners (e.g., articles, demonstratives). i. Use frequently occurring prepositions (e.g., *during, beyond, toward*). j. Produce and expand complete simple and compound declarative, interrogative, imperative, and exclamatory sentences in response to prompts.

continued

continued from previous

Speaking and Listening Standards	Language Standards
1 **SL.1.6:** Produce complete sentences when appropriate to task and situation. (See grade 1 Language standards 1 and 3 for specific expectations.)	**1** **L.1.6:** Use words and phrases acquired through conversations, reading and being read to, and responding to texts, including using frequently occurring conjunctions to signal simple relationships (e.g., *because*).
2 **SL.2.1:** Participate in collaborative conversations with diverse partners about grade 2 topics and texts with peers and adults in small and larger groups. a. Follow agreed-upon rules for discussions (e.g., gaining the floor in respectful ways listening to others with care, speaking one at a time about the topics and texts under discussion). b. Build on others' talk in conversations by linking their comments to the remarks of others. c. Ask for clarification and further explanation as needed about the topics and texts under discussion.	**2** **L.2.1:** Demonstrate command of the conventions of standard English grammar and usage when writing or speaking. a. Use collective nouns (e.g., *group*). b. Form and use frequently occurring irregular plural nouns (e.g., *feet, children, teeth, mice, fish*). c. Use reflexive pronouns (e.g., *myself, ourselves*). d. Form and use the past tense of frequently occurring irregular verbs (e.g., *sat, hid, told*). e. Use adjectives and adverbs and choose between them depending on what is to be modified. f. Produce, expand, and rearrange complete simple and compound sentences (e.g., *The boy watched the movie; The little boy watched the movie; The action movie was watched by the little boy*). g. Create readable documents with legible print.
2 **SL.2.6:** Produce complete sentences when appropriate to task and situation in order to provide requested detail or clarification. (See grade 2 Language standards 1 and 3 for specific expectations.)	**2** **L.2.3:** Use knowledge of language and its conventions when writing, speaking, reading, or listening. a. Compare formal and informal uses of English.
	2 **L.2.6:** Use words and phrases acquired through conversations, reading and being read to, and responding to texts, including using adjectives and adverbs to describe (e.g., *When other kids are happy that makes me happy*).

Source: *Common Core State Standards, K–12 English Language Arts* (2010).

Notes

What the **Teacher** Does

Teachers foster academic discourse skills when they establish routines and expectations for equitable and accountable conversations (e.g., Think-Pair-Share), carefully construct questions that promote extended content discussions (e.g., questions that students have sufficient background knowledge to discuss), and provide appropriate linguistic support (e.g., a sentence frame such as *"At school, I'm determined to _____ because_____.")*. Sentence frames are an ideal way to support young children to use academic vocabulary and increasingly complex sentence structures in meaningful ways as they discuss content and texts. With strategic scaffolding, all children learn to use English in ways that approach the more "literate" ways of communicating that are highly valued in school (Dutro & Kinsella, 2010; Gibbons, 2009; Merino & Scarcella, 2005; Schleppegrell, 2010) (ELA/ELD Framework, 2014, p. 211).

To offer opinions and ideas in conversations using a small set of learned phrases (e.g., *"I think _____"*), as well as open responses:

- Academic conversations should vary throughout the school year, and teachers should model for students how to have academic conversations for different purposes, including offering their opinions. Teachers can use sentence frames, in order to assist students with constructing their opinions and ensuring that they provide justifications for their thinking, instead of merely providing one or two words responses. Frames such as, *"In my opinion, _____"* and *"I think/believe that _____ because _____."* Students can begin with opinions about familiar topics such as their favorite ice cream or color, and then have more academic conversations such as their favorite character in a text that they read.

Participate in collaborative conversations with diverse partners about grade-appropriate topics and texts with peers and adults in small and larger groups:

- In order to teach active listening and turn-taking, teachers can have students use speaking and listening role cards with an ear for listening on one side and a mouth for speaking on the other. Each role card can also have frame for active listening (*"My partner said _____"* and for beginning a response, *"I think that _____"*).

- In order to continue a conversation through multiple exchanges, the teacher can require students to speak to multiple partners in the room, or have students use the text to justify and expand their responses. The teacher should also ask students to combine responses or come to consensus.

Produce complete sentences when appropriate to task and situation in order to provide requested detail or clarification:

- The teacher should provide students with sentence frames to begin their responses, which model for students how to produce appropriate grammatically and syntactically complete sentences. Students should also be asked to justify their responses using textual support, in order to provide requested detail or clarification. The teacher can model identifying textual support and incorporating it into her own response to provide more detail and clarification.

Tips for Differentiation by Proficiency Level

- *Emerging*—Students at the emerging level will need specific sentence frames for offering opinions, such as, *"I believe _____ because _____,"* as well as a word bank to complete their responses. Teachers will want to begin by using topics that students are familiar with, like their favorite food.

- *Expanding*—Students at the expanding level can begin to offer their opinions on academic topics, such as their favorite books. A more sophisticated sentence frame such as, *"In my opinion, _____ is best because _____."*

- *Bridging*—At the bridging level, students can begin to offer more detailed reasons that support their opinions, using a frame such as, *"I am convinced that _____. First, _____. Second, _____."* Students can also continue to discuss and expand upon academic topics.

Source: 2014 ELA/ELD Framework, p. 211.

Academic Vocabulary—Key Words and Phrases Related to Standard 3: Offering opinions

Accountable conversations: Empowering students to engage in discussions based on evidence. Students learn how to respect the views of their peers while strengthening their communication skills. They get practice in being good conversationalists by participating in conversations in a polite manner. An example of this is Think-Pair-Share.

Appropriate register: Referring to particular varieties or styles of speaking and writing. Registers vary because the language is used for different purposes, in different contexts, and for different audiences

Elaborating on an idea: Offering an opinion that builds upon the current conversation to expand the thinking. Effective elaborations include explanations with evidence as to their relevance to the conversation.

Gaining/holding the floor: Respectful and inclusive methods of assigning turns or using agreed-upon techniques so that students can enter into a group conversation, say their part, respond to questions if necessary, and then exit so that someone else can speak. Such methods should be part of the regular classroom norms of conduct or collaboration.

Negotiating with others: Within conversations, negotiating means the students are seeking to discover a common ground and reach an agreement to settle a mutual concern or resolve a disagreement. Negotiation may be about the conversation process itself, or about the subject being discussed. Negotiating tools include active listening, co-constructing of ideas, brainstorming, and 3-2-1 preference approaches.

Providing counterarguments: Offering an opinion that differs from what the current conversation seems to be saying. Effective counterarguments include explanations with evidence as to their relevance to the conversation.

Sentence frames: If students are struggling to find the right words to explain, describe, and clarify what they are thinking, a sentence starter or sentence frame helps them to get the idea started; for example, *"I think the statement is true because_____"* or *"This makes me wonder_____."* Sentence frames can be open ended or closed.

Using learned phrases: Using response prompts or stems to begin the student's contribution to a conversation, such as *"I think _____,"* *"I agree with _____,"* or *"That's a good idea, but_____"* Learned phrases help a student ease in to a conversation using a familiar pattern.

Using open responses: Beginning a student's contribution to a conversation without the use of learned phrases. Open responses may offer students a chance to contribute without the fixed beginning of a learned phrase.

Sources: Taberski & Burke, (2014), *The Common Core Companion: The Standards Decoded, Grades K–2.*

Notes

Example of Practice in Snapshot Related to Standard 3: Offering opinions

Snapshot 3.11. Expanding Sentences and Building Vocabulary Designated ELD Connected to ELA/Social Studies in Grade 1

Because Mr. Dupont's EL children are at the Bridging level of English language proficiency, during designated ELD, he provides his students with extended opportunities to discuss their ideas and opinions, as he knows that this will support them later when writing down their ideas. He strategically targets particular language that he would like students to use in their opinion pieces by constructing sentence frames that contain specific vocabulary and grammatical structures that will enable his students to be more precise and detailed (e.g., *My favorite hero is _____ because _____. _____ was very courageous when _____.*). He explains to the children how they can expand their ideas in different ways by adding information about where, when, how, and so forth. For example, he explains that instead of simply saying, *"She worked on a farm,"* children could say, *"She worked on a farm in California,"* or they could add even more detail and precision by saying, *"She worked on a farm in the central valley of California."* He provides his students with many opportunities to construct these expanded sentence structures as the students discuss the historical figures they are learning about and then write short summaries of their discussions at the end of each lesson. During these lessons, he encourages the children to refer to the texts they have previously read together and to cite evidence from them to support their ideas.

CA ELD Standards (Bridging): ELD.PI.K–1.1, 3, 6, 10, 12b; ELD.PII.K–1.4–5, 6
CA CCSS for ELA/Literacy: RI.1.1; SL.1.1, 4, 6; L.1.6

The snapshots and vignettes cited above can be found in their entirety at https://www.cde.ca.gov/ci/rl/cf/, *ELA/ELD Framework*, p. 260.

Notes

Notes

Emerging

K No standard for Kindergarten.

1 No standard for Grade 1.

2 Recognize that language choices (e.g., vocabulary) vary according to social setting (e.g., playground versus classroom), with substantial support from peers or adults.

Expanding

K No standard for Kindergarten.

1 No standard for Grade 1.

2 Adjust language choices (e.g., vocabulary, **use of dialogue, and so on) according to purpose (e.g., persuading, entertaining), task, and audience (e.g., peers versus adults)**, with **moderate support** from peers or adults.

Bridging

K No standard for Kindergarten.

1 No standard for Grade 1.

2 Adjust language choices according to purpose (e.g., persuading, entertaining), task, and audience (e.g., **peer-to-peer versus peer-to-teacher**), with **light support** from peers or adults.

Script *in bold italics* indicates content not found in earlier proficiency levels of the same ELD Standard.

Source: *California English Language Development Standards for Grades K–12*, California Department of Education (2012).

Notes

What the **Student** Does

Emerging

K No standard for Kindergarten.

1 No standard for Grade 1.

Expanding

K No standard for Kindergarten.

1 No standard for Grade 1.

Bridging

K No standard for Kindergarten.

1 No standard for Grade 1.

Gist: *Students adjust their vocabulary and use of dialogue according to purpose and audience, with some help from peers or adults.*

2 They consider:

- What do I really want to say?
- Who is my audience?

2 They *also* consider:

- Do I know the difference between informal and formal language when speaking?

2 They *also* consider:

- Do I know whether to use formal or informal language when speaking?

Source: *California English Language Development Standards for Grades K–12 (2012).*

Speaking and Listening Standards	Language Standards
K No standard for Kindergarten.	**K** No standard for Kindergarten.
1 No standard for Grade 1.	**1** No standard for Grade 1.
2 **SL.2.1:** Participate in collaborative conversations with diverse partners about grade 2 topics and texts with peers and adults in small and larger groups. a. Follow agreed-upon rules for discussions (e.g., gaining the floor in respectful ways listening to others with care, speaking one at a time about the topics and texts under discussion). b. Build on others' talk in conversations by linking their comments to the remarks of others. c. Ask for clarification and further explanation as needed about the topics and texts under discussion.	**2** **L.2.1:** Demonstrate command of the conventions of standard English grammar and usage when writing or speaking. a. Use collective nouns (e.g., *group*). b. Form and use frequently occurring irregular plural nouns (e.g., *feet, children, teeth, mice, fish*). c. Use reflexive pronouns (e.g., *myself, ourselves*). d. Form and use the past tense of frequently occurring irregular verbs (e.g., *sat, hid, told*). e. Use adjectives and adverbs, and choose between them depending on what is to be modified. f. Produce, expand, and rearrange complete simple and compound sentences (e.g., *The boy watched the movie; The little boy watched the movie; The action movie was watched by the little boy*). g. Create readable documents with legible print.
2 **SL.2.6:** Produce complete sentences when appropriate to task and situation in order to provide requested detail or clarification. (See grade 2 Language standards 1 and 3 for specific expectations.)	**2** **L.2.3:** Use knowledge of language and its conventions when writing, speaking, reading, or listening. a. Compare formal and informal uses of English.
	2 **L.2.6:** Use words and phrases acquired through conversations, reading and being read to, and responding to texts, including using adjectives and adverbs to describe (e.g., *When other kids are happy that makes me happy*).

In addition to the ELA Language and Speaking/Listening standards provided in this chart, this ELD Standard 4: Adapting language choices is **also** correlated with ELA Writing standards 2.4 and 2.5.

Source: *Common Core State Standards, K–12 English Language Arts* (2010).

What the **Teacher** Does

Students build language awareness as they come to understand how different text types use particular language resources (e.g., vocabulary, grammatical structures, ways of structuring and organizing whole texts). Language awareness is fostered when students have opportunities to experiment with language, shaping and enriching their own language using these language resources. During designated ELD instruction, children engage in discussions related to *the content knowledge* they are learning in ELA and other content areas, and these discussions promote the use of the language from those content areas. Students also *discuss the new language* they are learning to use. For example, students might learn about the grammatical structures of a particular complex text they are reading in science or ELA, or they might explicitly learn some of the general academic vocabulary used in the texts they are reading in ELA or social studies (2014 ELA/ELD Framework, p. 335).

Teachers can assist students with adapting language choices by recognizing that language choices (e.g., vocabulary) vary according to social setting (e.g., playground versus classroom), with substantial support from peers or adults:

- Teachers can assist students with adapting language choices by analyzing the specific language choices that authors have made. Using instructional read alouds, teachers can highlight key vocabulary or grammatical structures that the author has used for a variety of purposes, including persuasion, key vocabulary, or discussions.

- Teachers can also use contrastive analysis to demonstrate how students can adapt language according to the social setting that they are in. For example, *"Where you at?"* in a social setting can become *"Where are you?"* in an academic setting, or *"Where art thou?"* in Shakespearean English. A variety of these examples can be utilized to demonstrate register shifts.

- For more concrete examples, students can put on different kinds of hats or clothing, when using different kinds of language. For example, when using social language, a student can wear a baseball hat, and when using more formal language, a top hat can be used.

Tips for Differentiation by Proficiency Level

- *Emerging* —At the emerging stage, teachers can use think alouds to highlight the language choices that authors make with repetitive texts, and then chart those words or phrases for students on poster paper.

- *Expanding* —At the expanding level, students can begin to highlight key words or phrases that they notice in at first repetitive texts, and then more complex texts. Teachers can use sentence frames with these word choices so that students can begin to use them in both spoken and written language.

- *Bridging* —At the bridging level, different text types can be analyzed for key vocabulary or grammatical structures, and students can be asked to use those in their own writing.

Source: 2014 ELA/ELD Framework, p. 335.

Academic Vocabulary—Key Words and Phrases Related to Standard 4: Adapting language choices

Extended listening: Learning to successfully listen to increasingly longer texts.

Extensive listening: The ability to successfully listen to a wide range of texts.

Formal uses of English: Formal English is most commonly used in writing (reports, oral presentations, and essays) and less commonly in conversations. It uses longer sentences and academic vocabulary more frequently.

Informal uses of English: Informal English is found in everyday conversations and in personal correspondence (notes and letters, e-mails). It is likely to include idioms, contractions, and slang in short sentences and/or phrases.

Language choices: Choosing to use formal or informal English depending on the purpose of the conversation and the audience. Choices include use of vocabulary, use of dialogue, inclusion of idioms and slang, need for academic language, etc.

Purpose of entertaining: The speaker or writer is seeking to have listeners or readers enjoy what she or he is saying or writing. Examples include telling jokes, writing funny stories, or retelling an interesting experience. Informal English is usually used for the purpose of entertaining.

Purpose of persuading: The speaker or writer is seeking to influence the thinking of the listener or reader to be in agreement with the speaker or writer. Examples include first person essays, a literary response, debates, or op-ed pieces in the newspaper. Formal English is more often used for the purpose of persuading.

Think aloud: Teachers verbalizing aloud while reading a selection orally. Their verbalizations describing things they're doing as they read to monitor their comprehension. The purpose of the think-aloud strategy is to model for students how skilled readers construct meaning from a text.

Source: *Taberski & Burke, (2014), The Common Core Companion: The Standards Decoded, Grades K–2.*

Notes

Example of Practice in Snapshot Related to Standard 4: Adapting language choices

Vignette 3.5. Interactive Read Alouds With Informational Texts Integrated ELA, Literacy, and Science Instruction in Grade 1

Mrs. Fabian works with her students during designated ELD time to unpack sentences in other science texts she is using, focusing strategically on the aspects of the sentences that make them dense (e.g., long noun phrases, prepositional phrases). She uses a rubric based on the CA ELD Standards to assess how individual students are progressing with their use of particular language resources (e.g., vocabulary, grammatical structures, text organization). Whenever possible, she encourages them to use the new language, prompting them with questions like, *"How can you combine those two ideas to show they are happening at the same time?"* Although the children often produce imperfect sentences, Mrs. Fabian offers corrective feedback sparingly since she knows that the children are experimenting with language and practicing the grammatical structures that they will continue to learn as the unit progresses.

Primary CA CCSS for ELA/Literacy: RI.1.2—*Identify the main topic and retell key details of a text*; RI.1.3—*Describe the connection between two individuals, events, ideas, or pieces of information in a text*; RI.1.7—*Use the illustrations and details in a text to describe its key ideas*; W.1.7—*Participate in shared research and writing projects . . .*; SL.1.1—*Participate in collaborative conversations with diverse partners*; SL.1.2—*Ask and answer questions about key details in a text read aloud . . .*; L.1.6—*Use words and phrases acquired through conversations, reading and being read to, and responding to texts . . .*

CA ELD Standards (Expanding): ELD.PI.1—*Contribute to class, group, and partner discussions by listening attentively, following turn-taking rules, and asking and answering questions*; ELD.PI.5—*Demonstrate active listening to read-alouds and oral presentations by asking and answering questions with oral sentence frames and occasional prompting and support*; ELD.PI.11—*Offer opinions and provide good reasons and some textual evidence or relevant background knowledge (e.g., paraphrased examples from text or knowledge of content)*; ELD.PI.12b—*Use a growing number of general academic and domain-specific words . . .*

The snapshots and vignettes cited above can be found in their entirety at https://www.cde.ca.gov/ci/rl/cf/, *ELA/ELD Framework*, p. 263.

Notes

Part 1

INTERACTING IN MEANINGFUL WAYS

B *Interpretive Mode*

Introduction

Part I of the *California ELD Standards* promotes English Language Learners' abilities to *interact in meaningful ways* so that they acquire English and develop content knowledge simultaneously. Part I **comes first in the standards** to emphasize that students need to interact with adults and each other about meaning and content before they enter deeply into how the English language works. Part I, Interacting in Meaningful Ways, is subdivided into three clusters of standards that emphasize student participation in the major modes of communication: Collaborative, Interpretive, and Productive.

Cluster B: Interpretive Mode Standards have the same general descriptions K–12 for the four standards in the cluster, related to the comprehension and analysis of written and spoken texts. These include

1. *Listening actively to spoken English in a range of social and academic contexts.* Language is sometimes referred to as the "hidden curriculum" because it is not always specifically taught. Teachers can help students unlock this curriculum by making language features explicit through questioning of students as they are listening to spoken English (Christie, 1999).

2. *Reading closely literary and informational texts and viewing multimedia to determine how meaning is conveyed explicitly and implicitly through language.* These tasks often involve complex processes, including applying prior knowledge, making inferences, and resolving ambiguities (Acevedo & Rose, 2007; August & Shanahan, 2006).

3. *Evaluating how well writers and speakers use language to support ideas and opinions with details or reasons depending on modality, text type, purpose, audience, topic, and content area.* Formal (written-like registers) and informal (spoken-like registers) language use include domain-specific vocabulary, sentences and clauses packed with meaning, and whole texts that are cohesive (Christie & Derewianka, 2008; O'Dowd, 2010).

4. *Analyzing how writers and speakers use vocabulary and other language resources for specific purposes (to explain, persuade, entertain, etc.) depending on modality, text type, purpose, audience, topic, and content area.* Language resources, such as grammatical, lexical, and discourse features, interact with one another to help writers and speakers select the most appropriate methods of making meaning, depending on context and situation (Halliday & Matthiessen, 2004). Schleppegrell (2012) calls this "register variation," making choices about language based on purpose, audience, topic, and content area.

In *The California ELD Companion*, the What the Student Does section provides specific descriptions of competence with each of the Interpretive standards at the appropriate grade range and proficiency level. Similarly, the What the Teacher Does section provides specific strategies for developing competence with each of the Interpretive standards at the appropriate grade range. And the last section, Vignettes and Snapshots, offers classroom-level descriptions of what each standard looks like in practice.

Source: *California English Language Development Standards, K–12*, California Department of Education (2012). Chapter 4, "Theoretical Foundations and the Research Bases of the CA ELD Standards," provides an excellent summary of the research used in developing the four Interpretive standards in Part I, B.

Emerging

K Demonstrate active listening to read-alouds and oral presentations by asking and answering yes-no and wh- questions with oral sentence frames and substantial prompting and support.

1 Demonstrate active listening to read-alouds and oral presentations by asking and answering yes-no and wh- questions with oral sentence frames and substantial prompting and support.

2 Demonstrate active listening to read-alouds and oral presentations by asking and answering basic questions, with oral sentence frames and substantial prompting and support.

Expanding

K Demonstrate active listening to read-alouds and oral presentations by asking and answering questions with oral sentence frames and *occasional prompting and support*.

1 Demonstrate active listening to read-alouds and oral presentations by asking and answering questions, with oral sentence frames and *occasional prompting and support*.

2 Demonstrate active listening to read-alouds and oral presentations by asking and answering *detailed questions*, with oral sentence frames and *occasional prompting and support*.

Bridging

K Demonstrate active listening to read-alouds and oral presentations by asking and answering *detailed questions, with minimal prompting and light support*.

1 Demonstrate active listening to read-alouds and oral presentations by asking and answering *detailed questions, with minimal prompting and light support*.

2 Demonstrate active listening to read-alouds and oral presentations by asking and answering detailed questions, with *minimal prompting and light support*.

Script *in bold italics* indicates content not found in earlier proficiency levels of the same ELD Standard.

Source: *California English Language Development Standards for Grades K–12*, California Department of Education (2012).

Notes

What the **Student** Does

Emerging	Expanding	Bridging
Gist: *Students show active listening to read-alouds and oral presentations by asking and answering questions with oral sentence frames and some prompting and support.*		
K They consider:	K They *also* consider:	K They *also* consider:
• Do I understand most of what is being read aloud or presented to me? • What do I want to ask to understand this better? • Do I know how to get help to ask and answer questions?	• Can I use oral sentence frames so that others understand my question and/or answer?	• Can I ask and answer specific detailed questions with just a little help?
Gist: *Students show active listening to read-alouds and oral presentations by asking and answering questions with oral sentence frames and some prompting and support.*		
1 They consider:	1 They *also* consider:	1 They *also* consider:
• Do I understand most of what is being read aloud or presented to me? • What do I want to ask to understand this better? • Do I know how to get help to ask and answer questions?	• Can I use oral sentence frames so that others understand my question and/or answer? • What seems to be the most important parts of what I am hearing?	• Can I ask and answer specific detailed questions with just a little help? • What do I want to know more about after this story or presentation?
Gist: *Students show active listening to read-alouds and oral presentations by asking and answering questions with oral sentence frames and some prompting and support.*		
2 They consider:	2 They *also* consider:	2 They *also* consider:
• Do I understand most of what is being read aloud or presented to me? • What do I want to ask to understand this better? • Do I know how to get help to ask and answer questions?	• Can I use oral sentence frames so that others understand my question and/or answer? • What seems to be the most important parts of what I am hearing? • What can I do before, during, or after reading to help me better understand what I read?	• Can I ask and answer specific detailed questions with just a little help? • What do I want to know more about after this story or presentation? • Were there facts that surprised me or seemed different than what I already know about this?

Source: *California English Language Development Standards for Grades K–12 (2012).*

Speaking and Listening Standards	Language Standards
K **SL.K.1:** Participate in collaborative conversations with diverse partners about kindergarten topics and texts with peers and adults in small and larger groups. a. Follow agreed-upon rules for discussions (e.g., listening to others and taking turns speaking about the topics and texts under discussion). b. Continue a conversation through multiple exchanges.	
K **SL.K.2:** Confirm understanding of a text read aloud or information presented orally or through other media by asking and answering questions about key details and requesting clarification if something is not understood. a. Understand and follow one- and two-step oral directions.	
K **SL.K.3:** Ask and answer questions in order to seek help, get information, or clarify something that is not understood.	
1 **SL.1.1:** Participate in collaborative conversations with diverse partners about grade 1 topics and texts with peers and adults in small and larger groups. a. Follow agreed-upon rules for discussions (e.g., listening to others with care, speaking one at a time about the topics and texts under discussion). b. Build on others' talk in conversations by responding to the comments of others through multiple exchanges. c. Ask questions to clear up any confusion about the topics and texts under discussion.	
1 **SL.1.2:** Ask and answer questions about key details in a text read aloud or information presented orally or through other media. a. Give, restate, and follow simple two-step directions.	

continued

continued from previous

Speaking and Listening Standards	Language Standards
1 **SL.1.3:** Ask and answer questions about what a speaker says in order to gather additional information or clarify something that is not understood.	
2 **SL.2.1:** Participate in collaborative conversations with diverse partners about grade 2 topics and texts with peers and adults in small and larger groups. a. Follow agreed-upon rules for discussions (e.g., gaining the floor in respectful ways listening to others with care, speaking one at a time about the topics and texts under discussion). b. Build on others' talk in conversations by linking their comments to the remarks of others. c. Ask for clarification and further explanation as needed about the topics and texts under discussion.	**2** **L.2.3:** Use knowledge of language and its conventions when writing, speaking, reading, or listening. a. Compare formal and informal uses of English.
2 **SL.2.2:** Recount or describe key ideas or details from a text read aloud or information presented orally or through other media. a. Give and follow three- and four-step oral directions.	
2 **SL.2.3:** Ask and answer questions about what a speaker says in order to clarify comprehension, gather additional information, or deepen understanding of a topic or issue.	

Source: *Common Core State Standards, K–12 English Language Arts* (2010).

Notes

What the **Teacher** Does

Effective discussions do not just happen. They require a skillful teacher who teaches children *how* to engage in discussions with peers and others. Part of having effective discussions is learning to actively listen. Students in the primary grades may want to focus more on their own thoughts and ideas and will need to be explicitly taught *how* to actively listen.

Teachers can assist students with demonstrating active listening to read alouds and oral presentations by asking and answering yes/no and why questions with oral sentence frames and varying levels of support by

- Active listening is a scaffold for reading (Soto, 2012). Just as everyone can read in different ways, close readings or reading for overall comprehension, students must be explicitly taught how to listen actively and for what purpose. Students can practice listening for specific information or the gist. The teacher should model how to actively listen, either with another student or an adult, so that students understand *how* to paraphrase and listen carefully to their partner's response.

- Demonstrate discussion behaviors that indicate respect for others, such as listening closely, not interrupting, responding to comments, encouraging others to contribute, and acknowledging and appreciating all participants' thinking on the topic. Students can be taught the three Ls of listening: Look, Lean, and Listen. They can physically practice these behaviors so that they know the expectations for listening.

- Explain effective contributions to discussions, such as comments that are related to the topic, and build on others' remarks and questions that serve to clarify or that request elaboration (i.e., staying on topic) (*2014 ELA/ELD Framework*, p. 210).

Tips for Differentiation by Proficiency Level

- *Emerging*—At the emerging level and in the primary grades, students can be given listening role cards with an ear on them that have been photocopied in red, so that students know that they should stop and listen to their partner. On the backside of the role card, sentence frames for active listening can be printed, such as, "*My partner said _____*" or "*What I'm hearing you say is _____.*"

- *Expanding*—At the expanding level, students can begin to ask clarifying questions, as well as requests for more information, after listening to their partner or a presentation.

- *Bridging*—At the bridging level, students can begin to provide more detailed information regarding what their partner said or a presentation. They can use more complex frames such as, "*In other words, _____. This is important because _____.*"

Source: *2014 ELA/ELD Framework*, p. 210.

Academic Vocabulary—Key Words and Phrases Related to Standard 5: Listening actively

Active listening: Paying attention to a read-aloud or oral presentation with a sense of purpose, such as a focus question. The teacher may signal purpose by saying, *"Listen for what the boy says in the story that tells us _____."* Active listening may include taking notes, drawing what the student is hearing, partner talk on understanding the gist, and collaborative classroom discussion.

Extensive (wide) reading: Reading texts within a wide range of genres.

Instructional read-alouds: Using an anchor text as the basis for gathering deep meaning, with the teacher conducting a "close reading" of a text. This includes multiple readings of the text over time, allowing students to know it well, and to internalize its language, syntax, and meaning. This is not the single, simple reading of a story by the teacher. Teachers intentionally focus the reading, asking text-dependent questions that help students build vocabulary and knowledge from the text.

Oral sentence frames: Using simple phrases to signal what the student may say and to make conversations more respectful and productive. They should be a consistent pattern in discussions, giving students a familiar way to add their contributions positively. Common sentence frames include *"I think X is true because _____,"* *"I agree with _____'s idea because _____,"* or *"I made a connection between _____ and _____."*

Source: Taberski & Burke, (2014), *The Common Core Companion: The Standards Decoded, Grades K–2.*

Notes

Example of Practice in Snapshot Related to Standard 5: Listening actively

Vignette 3.5. Interactive Read Alouds With Informational Texts Integrated ELA, Literacy, and Science Instruction in Grade 1

Mrs. Fabian: Wow! I can tell you already know a lot about bees. Today, we are going to learn something new. We are going to reread a couple of pages in one book we've been reading, *The Honeymakers*, by Gail Gibbons. As you listen, I'd like you to think about what the main ideas is in this section. What is it mostly about? (Reading from a passage midway through the book) *"At each flower the forager bee collects nectar with her proboscis. She stores the nectar in a special part of her body called the crop, or honey stomach. This stomach is separate from her other stomach "* (2014 ELA/ELD Framework, p. 265).

Mrs. Fabian: That's good evidence that tells me what this section is mostly about. Children, listen carefully as I reread this part so that we can make sure we're getting the main idea (rereads the passage). Thumbs up or down everyone if you agree that this part is mostly about the bees collecting nectar and storing it in their honey stomachs.

Primary CA CCSS for ELA/Literacy: RI.1.2—Identify the main topic and retell key details of a text; RI.1.3—Describe the connection between two individuals, events, ideas, or pieces of information in a text; RI.1.7—Use the illustrations and details in a text to describe its key ideas; W.1.7—Participate in shared research and writing projects . . . ; SL.1.1—Participate in collaborative conversations with diverse partners; SL.1.2—Ask and answer questions about key details in a text read aloud . . . ; L.1.6—Use words and phrases acquired through conversations, reading and being read to, and responding to texts . . .

CA ELD Standards (Expanding): ELD.PI.1—Contribute to class, group, and partner discussions by listening attentively, following turn-taking rules, and asking and answering questions; ELD.PI.5—Demonstrate active listening to read-alouds and oral presentations by asking and answering questions with oral sentence frames and occasional prompting and support; ELD.PI.11—Offer opinions and provide good reasons and some textual evidence or relevant background knowledge (e.g., paraphrased examples from text or knowledge of content); ELD.PI.12b—Use a growing number of general academic and domain-specific words . . .

The snapshots and vignettes cited above can be found in their entirety at https://www.cde.ca.gov/ci/rl/cf/, *ELA/ELD Framework*, p. 265.

Notes

Notes

Emerging

K Describe ideas, phenomena (e.g., parts of a plant), and text elements (e.g., characters) based on understanding of a select set of grade-level texts and viewing of multimedia, with substantial support.

1 Describe ideas, phenomena (e.g., plant life cycle), and text elements (e.g., characters) based on understanding of a select set of grade-level texts and viewing of multimedia, with substantial support.

2 Describe ideas, phenomena (e.g., plant life cycle), and text elements (e.g., main idea, characters, events) based on understanding of a select set of grade-level texts and viewing of multimedia, with substantial support.

Expanding

K Describe ideas, phenomena (e.g., how butterflies eat), and text elements (e.g., *setting*, characters) *in greater detail* based on understanding of a *variety* of grade-level texts and viewing of multimedia, with *moderate support*.

1 Describe ideas, phenomena (e.g., how earthworms eat), and text elements (*e.g., setting, main idea*) *in greater detail* based on understanding of a *variety* of grade-level texts and viewing of multimedia, with *moderate support*.

2 Describe ideas, phenomena (e.g., how earthworms eat), and text elements (*e.g., setting*, events) *in greater detail* based on understanding of a *variety* of grade-level texts and viewing of multimedia, with *moderate support*.

Bridging

K Describe ideas, phenomena (e.g., insect metamorphosis), and text elements (e.g., *major events*, characters, setting) *using key details* based on understanding of a variety of grade-level texts and viewing of multimedia, with *light support*.

1 Describe ideas, phenomena (e.g., erosion), and text elements (*e.g., central message, character traits*) *using key details* based on understanding of a variety of grade-level texts and viewing of multimedia, with *light support*.

2 Describe ideas, phenomena (e.g., erosion), and text elements (*e.g., central message, character traits*) *using key details* based on understanding of a variety of grade-level texts and viewing of multimedia, with *light support*.

Script *in bold italics* indicates content not found in earlier proficiency levels of the same ELD Standard.

Source: *California English Language Development Standards for Grades K–12*, California Department of Education (2012).

Notes

What the **Student** Does

Emerging	Expanding	Bridging
Gist: *Students describe ideas, science concepts, and text elements in some detail by understanding grade-level texts and viewing of multimedia, with some support.*		
K They consider: • Who or what is this text mostly about? • What do I already know about this topic?	**K** They *also* consider: • What is the main topic of this text? • How do the details in the text help me understand the setting and major events?	**K** Same as Expanding.
Gist: *Students describe ideas, science concepts, and text elements in greater detail by understanding grade-level texts and viewing of multimedia, with some support.*		
1 They consider: • Who or what is this text mostly about? • What do I already know about this topic?	**1** They *also* consider: • What is the main topic of this text? • How do the details in the text help me understand the setting and major events?	**1** Same as Expanding.
Gist: *Students describe ideas, science concepts, and text elements in greater detail by understanding grade-level texts and viewing of multimedia, with some support.*		
2 They consider: • Do I understand most of what is being read aloud or presented to me?	**2** They *also* consider: • What are the most important details that I need to remember?	**2** They *also* consider: • What information or message does the author want me to understand from this text? • What key details help me to know this?

Source: *California English Language Development Standards for Grades K–12 (2012).*

Speaking and Listening Standards	Language Standards
K **SL.K.2:** Confirm understanding of a text read aloud or information presented orally or through other media by asking and answering questions about key details and requesting clarification if something is not understood. a. Understand and follow one- and two-step oral directions.	**K** **L.K.4:** Determine or clarify the meaning of unknown and multiple-meaning words and phrases based on kindergarten reading and content. a. Identify new meanings for familiar words and apply them accurately (e.g., knowing duck is a bird and learning the verb to duck). b. Use the most frequently occurring inflections and affixes (e.g., *-ed, -s, re-, un-, pre-, -ful, -less*) as a clue to the meaning of an unknown word.
K **SL.K. 3:** Ask and answer questions in order to seek help, get information, or clarify something that is not understood.	**K** **L.K.6:** Use words and phrases acquired through conversations, reading and being read to, and responding to texts.
1 **SL.1.2:** Ask and answer questions about key details in a text read aloud or information presented orally or through other media. a. Give, restate, and follow simple two-step directions.	**1** **L.1.4:** Determine or clarify the meaning of unknown and multiple-meaning words and phrases based on grade 1 reading and content, choosing flexibly from an array of strategies. a. Use sentence-level context as a clue to the meaning of a word or phrase. b. Use frequently occurring affixes as a clue to the meaning of a word. c. Identify frequently occurring root words (e.g., *look*) and their inflectional forms (e.g., *looks, looked, looking*).
1 **SL.1.3:** Ask and answer questions about what a speaker says in order to gather additional information or clarify something that is not understood.	**1** **L.1.6:** Use words and phrases acquired through conversations, reading and being read to, and responding to texts, including using frequently occurring conjunctions to signal simple relationships (e.g., *because*).
2 **SL.2.2:** Recount or describe key ideas or details from a text read aloud or information presented orally or through other media. a. Give and follow three- and four-step oral directions.	**2** **L.2.3:** Use knowledge of language and its conventions when writing, speaking, reading, or listening. a. Compare formal and informal uses of English.

continued

continued from previous

Speaking and Listening Standards	Language Standards
2 **SL.2.3:** Ask and answer questions about what a speaker says in order to clarify comprehension, gather additional information, or deepen understanding of a topic or issue.	**2** **L.2.4:** Determine or clarify the meaning of unknown and multiple-meaning words and phrases based on grade 2 reading and content, choosing flexibly from an array of strategies. a. Use sentence-level context as a clue to the meaning of a word or phrase. b. Determine the meaning of the new word formed when a known prefix is added to a known word (e.g., *happy/unhappy, tell/retell*). c. Use a known root word as a clue to the meaning of an unknown word with the same root (e.g., *addition, additional*). d. Use knowledge of the meaning of individual words to predict the meaning of compound words (e.g., *birdhouse, lighthouse, housefly; bookshelf, notebook, bookmark*). e. Use glossaries and beginning dictionaries, both print and digital, to determine or clarify the meaning of words and phrases in all content areas.
	2 **L.2.6:** Use words and phrases acquired through conversations, reading and being read to, and responding to texts, including using adjectives and adverbs to describe (e.g., *When other kids are happy that makes me happy*).

In addition to the CCSS ELA Language and Speaking Listening standards listed in the chart, ELD Standard 6 Reading/viewing closely is **also** correlated with ELA Reading Literature and Information standards K.1–7, 9–10, 1.1–7, 9–10, and 2.1–7, 9–10.

Source: *Common Core State Standards, K–12 English Language Arts* (2010).

Notes

What the **Teacher** Does

Comprehension is the focus of read aloud experiences with literary and informational text. Children ask and answer questions (RL/RI.1.1), with special, but not exclusive, emphasis on text-dependent questions, particularly those that demand higher-level thinking. They retell stories or information, identify the central message or main topic, and describe story elements (characters, settings, major events) and information (RL/RI.1.2–3). They learn about the craft and structure of literary and informational text, shifting their attention from meaning to how meaning is conveyed as they identify words that evoke feelings or use text features to locate information; explain differences between different genres and the purposes of various text features (glossaries, icons, headings); and identify the source of the story (the voice) or information (images or text) (RL/RI.1.4–6). They also attend to illustrations and details to describe characters, settings, and events, or key ideas, and they compare and contrast the adventures and experiences of characters and of two texts on the same topic (RL/RI.1.7, 9). Teachers provide systematic instruction in comprehension to ensure that children understand, enjoy, and learn from texts that are being read aloud (*2014 ELA/ELD Framework*, p. 239).

Teachers can assist students with describing ideas, phenomena (e.g., parts of a plant), and text elements (e.g., characters) based on understanding of a select set of grade-level texts and viewing of multimedia, by

- Modeling key comprehension skills such as summarizing, in order to read or closely view segments of texts. Teachers can demonstrate how to summarize the most important points, using an instructional read aloud and think aloud, in order that students understand how the main topic and key details are distilled from a text. Students can then discuss their summaries with each other.

- Using an Elmo projector can be used to show students how main ideas were highlighted from a text. One highlighter can be used for the main topic and another color for details.

- Using sentence frames such as "*I already know _____ about the topic*" or "*I learned _____ and _____ about the topic*" (see more below), have students engage in conversations with each other about ideas, phenomena, or text elements. Have students evaluate each other's close reading descriptions using a teacher-generated and grade-appropriate rubric.

Tips for Differentiation by Proficiency Level

- *Emerging*—At the emerging level, students can use sentence frames to discuss ideas, phenomena, or text elements. Sentence frames such as, "*This text is mostly about _____*" can be used.

- *Expanding*—At the expanding level, more complex sentence frames such as, "*The main topic of the text includes _____*" can be used in order to explain what was read closely.

- *Bridging*—At the bridging level, students can use evidence from the text with the frame, "*The key details that helped me to know this are _____ and _____.*" This frame allows students to provide more details around their thinking.

Source: *2014 ELA/ELD Framework*, p. 239.

Academic Vocabulary—Key Words and Phrases Related to Standard 6: Reading/viewing closely

Characters: Characters can be simple or complex, but those that are complex make some kind of change during the text, and interact with others and their environments.

Close reading: Reading that emphasizes the deeper meaning and larger connections between words, sentence, and the text; also paying attention to the author's organization, word choice, and style.

Key details: The parts of a text that support the main idea and enable the reader to draw conclusions or infer what the text is about.

Major events: The most important events in a story, usually related to how the main character resolves a problem or handles a challenge.

Prompting and support: Helping students to initiate or strengthen a particular or strategy, often by thinking aloud and modeling.

Setting: The time and place in which a story takes place. Students need to describe where it takes place and when it takes place.

Text: Usually means something being read (poem, essay, story, article), but can also mean more broadly an image, artwork, speech, or multimedia piece (website, film, etc.).

Text-dependent questions: Referring to questions asked by the teacher or others that require a familiarity with a specific text in order to be answered. Students cannot use general background knowledge or familiarity with other stories to respond to these questions.

Source: Taberski & Burke, (2014), *The Common Core Companion: The Standards Decoded, Grades K–2.*

Notes

Example of Practice in Snapshot Related to Standard 6: Reading/viewing closely

Vignette 4.1. Close Reading of *Lilly's Purple Plastic Purse* (Narrative Text) ELA Instruction in Grade 2

Today, Mrs. Hernandez is working with a small reading group of six children (two are ELLs at the Bridging level, two are bilingual students who are not ELLs, and two are native speakers of English only). They are reading *Lilly's Purple Plastic Purse*. Mrs. Hernandez helps students read the text closely by thinking about and discussing text-dependent questions. Yesterday, when the group read the book for the first time, Mrs. Hernandez asked text-dependent questions focused on literal comprehension. Today, she will stop at strategic points in the text and guide the children to discuss text-dependent questions targeting inferential comprehension of the text.

Primary CA CCSS for ELA/Literacy Addressed:

RL.2.1—Ask and answer such questions as who, what, where, when, why, and how to demonstrate understanding of key details in a text; RL.2.3—Describe how characters in a story respond to major events and challenges; W.2.1—Write opinion pieces in which they introduce the topic or book they are writing about, state an opinion, supply reasons that support the opinion, use linking words (e.g., because, and, also) to connect opinion and reasons, and provide a concluding statement or section; SL.2.1—Participate in collaborative conversations with diverse partners . . .

Primary CA ELD Standards Addressed (Bridging):

ELD.PI.1—Contribute to class, group, and partner discussions, including sustained dialogue, by listening attentively, following turn-taking rules, asking relevant questions, affirming others, adding pertinent information, building on responses, and providing useful feedback; ELD.PI.3—Offer opinions and negotiate with others in conversations . . . ; ELD.PI.6—Describe ideas, phenomena (e.g., erosion), and text elements (e.g., central message, character traits) using key details based on understanding of a variety of grade-level texts . . . with light support; ELD.PI.11—Support opinions or persuade others by providing good reasons and detailed textual evidence . . .

The snapshots and vignettes cited above can be found in their entirety at https://www.cde.ca.gov/ci/rl/cf/, *ELA/ELD Framework*, p. 341.

Notes

Notes

Emerging

K Describe the language an author uses to present an idea (e.g., the words and phrases used when a character is introduced), with prompting and substantial support.

1 Describe the language writers or speakers use to present an idea (e.g., the words and phrases used to describe a character), with prompting and substantial support.

2 Describe the language writers or speakers use to present an idea (e.g., the words and phrases used to describe a character), with prompting and substantial support.

Expanding

K Describe the language an author uses to present an idea *(e.g., the adjectives used to describe a character)*, with prompting and *moderate support*

1 Describe the language writers or speakers use to present *or support* an idea *(e.g., the adjectives used to describe people and places)*, with prompting and *moderate support.*

2 Describe the language writers or speakers use to present *or support* an idea *(e.g., the author's choice of vocabulary or phrasing to portray characters, places, or real people)*, with prompting and *moderate support.*

Bridging

K Describe the language an author uses to present *or support an idea (e.g., the vocabulary used to describe people and places)*, with prompting and *light support.*

1 Describe the language writers or speakers use to present or support an idea *(e.g., the author's choice of vocabulary to portray characters, places, or real people)* with prompting and *light support.*

2 Describe *how well* writers or speakers *use specific language resources* to support an opinion or present an idea *(e.g., whether the vocabulary used to present evidence is strong enough)*, with *light support.*

Script *in bold italics* indicates content not found in earlier proficiency levels of the same ELD Standard.

Source: *California English Language Development Standards for Grades K–12*, California Department of Education (2014).

Notes

What the **Student** Does

Emerging	Expanding	Bridging
Gist: *Students describe the language an author uses to present an idea with prompting and some support.*		
K They consider: • Who or what is this text mostly about? • What words does the author use to describe this main idea?	**K** They *also* consider: • Do I recognize the adjectives being used to describe a character?	**K** They *also* consider: • Do I recognize the adjectives being used to describe people and places?
Gist: *Students describe the language that writers or speakers use to present or support an idea with prompting and some support.*		
1 They consider: • Who or what is this text mostly about? • What words does the author or speaker use to describe this main idea?	**1** They *also* consider: • Do I recognize the adjectives being used to describe people and places?	**1** They *also* consider: • Do I recognize the adjectives being used to describe characters, places, or real people?
Gist: *Students describe how well the writers or speakers use language resources to present or support an idea with prompting and some support.*		
2 They consider: • Who or what is this text mostly about? • What words does the author or speaker use to describe this main idea?	**2** They *also* consider: • Do I recognize the adjectives being used to describe characters, places, or real people?	**2** They *also* consider: • How well does the writer or speaker use language to support an idea or opinion? • Does the vocabulary seem strong enough to support that idea or opinion?

Source: *California English Language Development Standards for Grades K–12 (2012).*

Speaking and Listening Standards	Language Standards
	K **L.K.4:** Determine or clarify the meaning of unknown and multiple-meaning words and phrases based on kindergarten reading and content. a. Identify new meanings for familiar words and apply them accurately (e.g., knowing duck is a bird and learning the verb to duck). b. Use the most frequently occurring inflections and affixes (e.g., *-ed, -s, re-, un-, pre-, -ful, -less*) as a clue to the meaning of an unknown word.
	K **L.K.5:** With guidance and support from adults, explore word relationships and nuances in word meanings. a. Sort common objects into categories (e.g., shapes, foods) to gain a sense of the concepts the categories represent. b. Demonstrate understanding of frequently occurring verbs and adjectives by relating them to their opposites (antonyms). c. Identify real-life connections between words and their use (e.g., note places at school that are colorful). d. Distinguish shades of meaning among verbs describing the same general action (e.g., *walk, march, strut, prance*) by acting out the meanings.
	K **L.K.6:** Use words and phrases acquired through conversations, reading and being read to, and responding to texts.
	1 **L.1.4:** Determine or clarify the meaning of unknown and multiple-meaning words and phrases based on grade 1 reading and content, choosing flexibly from an array of strategies. a. Use sentence-level context as a clue to the meaning of a word or phrase. b. Use frequently occurring affixes as a clue to the meaning of a word. c. Identify frequently occurring root words (e.g., *look*) and their inflectional forms (e.g., *looks, looked, looking*).
	1 **L.1.5:** With guidance and support from adults, demonstrate understanding of word relationships and nuances in word meanings. a. Sort words into categories (e.g., colors, clothing) to gain a sense of the concepts the categories represent. b. Define words by category and by one or more key attributes (e.g., *a duck is a bird that swims; a tiger is a large cat with stripes*).

continued

continued from previous

Speaking and Listening Standards	Language Standards
	c. Identify real-life connections between words and their use (e.g., note places at home that are cozy). d. Distinguish shades of meaning among verbs differing in manner (e.g., *look, peek, glance, stare, glare, scowl*) and adjectives differing in intensity (e.g., *large, gigantic*) by defining or choosing them or by acting out the meanings.
	1 **L.1.6:** Use words and phrases acquired through conversations, reading and being read to, and responding to texts, including using frequently occurring conjunctions to signal simple relationships (e.g., *because*).
2 **SL.2.3:** Ask and answer questions about what a speaker says in order to clarify comprehension, gather additional information, or deepen understanding of a topic or issue.	**2** **L.2.3:** Use knowledge of language and its conventions when writing, speaking, reading, or listening. a. Compare formal and informal uses of English.
	2 **L.2.4:** Determine or clarify the meaning of unknown and multiple-meaning words and phrases based on grade 2 reading and content, choosing flexibly from an array of strategies. a. Use sentence-level context as a clue to the meaning of a word or phrase. b. Determine the meaning of the new word formed when a known prefix is added to a known word (e.g., *happy/unhappy, tell/retell*). c. Use a known root word as a clue to the meaning of an unknown word with the same root (e.g., *addition, additional*). d. Use knowledge of the meaning of individual words to predict the meaning of compound words (e.g., *birdhouse, lighthouse, housefly; bookshelf, notebook, bookmark*). e. Use glossaries and beginning dictionaries, both print and digital, to determine or clarify the meaning of words and phrases in all content areas.
	2 **L.2.5:** Demonstrate understanding of word relationships and nuances in word meanings. a. Identify real-life connections between words and their use (e.g., describe foods that are spicy or juicy). b. Distinguish shades of meaning among closely related verbs (e.g., *toss, throw, hurl*) and closely related adjectives (e.g., *thin, slender, skinny, scrawny*).
	2 **L.2.6:** Use words and phrases acquired through conversations, reading and being read to, and responding to texts, including using adjectives and adverbs to describe (e.g., *When other kids are happy that makes me happy*).

In addition to the CCSS ELA Language and Speaking Listening standards listed in the chart, ELD Standard 7 Evaluating language choices is **also** correlated with ELA Reading Literature standards K.3–4, 6, 1.3–4, 6, and 2.3–4, 6 and Reading Information standards K.2, 6, 8, 1.2, 6, 8, and 2.2, 6, and 8.

Source: *Common Core State Standards, K–12 English Language Arts* (2010).

What the **Teacher** Does

As the foundation of literacy and all learning (and social competence), language development is crucial, particularly academic language. Children's language expands considerably as they engage with texts and learn to discuss and communicate their ideas and questions about texts, experiences, and concepts (2014 ELA/ELD Framework, p. 204).

Teachers can assist students with describing the language an author uses to present an idea (e.g., the words and phrases used when a character is introduced), with prompting, by

- Using texts that they have read to students during instructional read alouds to evaluate the language choices of authors. They can chart language that is repeated or key vocabulary that has been used in texts that have been read.

- Rereading familiar texts and having students identify adjectives to describe people and places.

- Having students identify the main idea of a familiar text by analyzing the words that author uses. Student can talk to each other about this, and then create a class list of key vocabulary used.

- After reading several texts by the same author, students can identify the similar language choices that the author makes across reading selections. As a class, the teacher can chart language choices used by the author.

- Based on the text, lead the class in a classroom discussion regarding whether an author used strong enough vocabulary to support an idea or opinion. Students can be asked to focus on the adjectives used to describe the character (e.g., *considerate, thoughtful, brave*), or words the author used to describe the main idea (e.g., most important idea, supporting details or facts, examples). Students can then offer additional suggestions to strengthen vocabulary.

Tips for Differentiation by Proficiency Level

- *Emerging*—At the emerging level, students can use the sentence frame, *"The words that the author uses to describe the main idea are _____."* Teachers can use sentence strips with key sentences from the text, as well as key vocabulary, so that they can model adjusting language choices.

- *Expanding*—At the expanding level, students can be given sentence strips with key sentences from the text, as well as key vocabulary, so that they can adjust language choices themselves. Students at this level can also use a sentence frame such as, *"The adjectives being used to describe people include _____."*

- *Bridging*—At the bridging level, students can be asked to adjust language choices by rewriting a text, using a sentence frame such as, *"The author could have used stronger language by using _____ vocabulary because _____."* Students could also be asked to rewrite a text using key vocabulary.

Source: 2014 ELA/ELD Framework, p. 204.

Academic Vocabulary—Key Words and Phrases Related to Standard 7: Evaluating language choices

Characters: Characters can be simple or complex, but those that are complex make some kind of change during the text and interact with others and their environments.

Key details: The parts of a text that support the main idea and enable the reader to draw conclusions or infer what the text is about.

Language choices: Choosing to use formal or informal English depending on the purpose of the conversation, the task at hand, and the audience. Choices include use of vocabulary, use of dialogue, inclusion of idioms and slang, need for academic language, etc.

Major events: The most important events in a story, usually related to how the main character resolves a problem or handles a challenge.

Prompting and support: Helping students to initiate or strengthen a particular or strategy, often by thinking aloud and modeling.

Sources: Taberski & Burke, (2014), *The Common Core Companion: The Standards Decoded, Grades K–2.*

Notes

Example of Practice in Snapshot Related to Standard 7: Evaluating language choices

Vignette 3.6. Unpacking Sentences Designated ELD Instruction in Grade 1

Mrs. Fabian works with her students during designated ELD time to unpack sentences in other science texts she is using, focusing strategically on the aspects of the sentences that make them dense (e.g., long noun phrases, prepositional phrases). She uses a rubric based on the CA ELD Standards to assess how individual students are progressing with their use of particular language resources (e.g., vocabulary, grammatical structures, text organization). Whenever possible, she encourages them to use the new language, prompting them with questions like, *"How can you combine those two ideas to show they are happening at the same time?"* Although the children often produce imperfect sentences, Mrs. Fabian offers corrective feedback sparingly since she knows that the children are experimenting with language and practicing the grammatical structures that they will continue to learn as the unit progresses.

CA ELD Standards (Expanding): ELD.PI.1—Contribute to class, group, and partner discussions by listening attentively, following turn-taking rules, and asking and answering questions; ELD.PI.7—Describe the language writers or speakers use to present or support an idea (e.g., the adjectives used to describe people and places) with prompting and moderate support; ELD.PII.6—Combine clauses in an increasing variety of ways to make connections between and to join ideas, for example, to express cause/effect (e.g., She jumped because the dog barked.), in shared language activities guided by the teacher and with increasing independence.

The snapshots and vignettes cited above can be found in their entirety at https://www.cde.ca.gov/ci/rl/cf/, *ELA/ELD Framework*, pp. 270–271.

Notes

Notes

Emerging

K Distinguish how two different frequently used words (e.g., describing an action with the verb *walk* versus *run*) produce a different effect.

1 Distinguish how two different frequently used words (e.g., *large* versus *small*) produce a different effect on the audience.

2 Distinguish how two different frequently used words (e.g., describing a character as *happy* versus *angry*) produce a different effect on the audience.

Expanding

K Distinguish how two different words *with similar meaning (e.g., describing an action as walk versus march) produce shades of meaning* and a different effect.

1 Distinguish how two different words *with similar meaning (e.g., large versus enormous) produce shades of meaning* and a different effect on the audience.

2 Distinguish how two different words *with similar meaning (e.g., describing a character as happy versus ecstatic) produce shades of meaning* and different effects on the audience.

Bridging

K Distinguish how *multiple* different words with similar meaning (e.g., *walk, march, strut, prance*) produce shades of meaning and a different effect.

1 *Distinguish how multiple* different words with similar meaning (e.g., *big, large, huge, enormous, gigantic*) produce shades of meaning and a different effect on the audience.

2 Distinguish how *multiple* different words with similar meaning (e.g., *pleased versus happy versus ecstatic, heard or knew versus believed*) produce shades of meaning and different effects on the audience.

Script *in bold italics* indicates content not found in earlier proficiency levels of the same ELD Standard.

Source: *California English Language Development Standards for Grades K–12*, California Department of Education (2012).

Notes

What the **Student** Does

Emerging	Expanding	Bridging

Gist: *Students can distinguish how two different words with similar meaning can produce a different effect.*

K They consider:

- Can I tell the difference between verbs that describe the same general action (e.g., *walking* and *running*)?

K They *also* consider:

- Can I see how using one word similar but different from another changes the meaning slightly?

K They *also* consider:

- Do I know the difference between words of similar meaning?
- How does the choice of one word instead of another make a difference to the meaning of a text?

Gist: *Students can distinguish how two different words with similar meaning can produce slightly different meaning and a different effect on the audience.*

1 They consider:

- Can I tell the difference between verbs that describe the same general action (e.g., *walking* and *running*)?

1 They *also* consider:

- Can I see how using one word similar but different from another changes the meaning slightly?

1 They *also* consider:

- Do I know the difference between words of similar meaning?
- How does the choice of one word instead of another make a difference to the meaning of a text?

Gist: *Students can distinguish how multiple different words with similar meaning can produce slightly different meaning and a different effect on the audience.*

2 They consider:

- Can I tell the difference between verbs that describe the same general action (e.g., *walking* and *running*)?

2 They *also* consider:

- Can I tell the difference between verbs that describe the same general action (e.g., *walking* and *running*)?
- Can I recognize how some adjectives change the meaning of a text by their intensity (*big* vs. *enormous*)?

2 They *also* consider:

- Do I know the difference between words of similar meaning?
- How does the choice of one word instead of another make a difference to the meaning of a text?

Speaking and Listening Standards	Language Standards
	K **L.K.4:** Determine or clarify the meaning of unknown and multiple-meaning words and phrases based on kindergarten reading and content. a. Identify new meanings for familiar words and apply them accurately (e.g., knowing duck is a bird and learning the verb to duck). b. Use the most frequently occurring inflections and affixes (e.g., *-ed, -s, re-, un-, pre-, -ful, -less*) as a clue to the meaning of an unknown word.
	K **L.K.5:** With guidance and support from adults, explore word relationships and nuances in word meanings. a. Sort common objects into categories (e.g., shapes, foods) to gain a sense of the concepts the categories represent. b. Demonstrate understanding of frequently occurring verbs and adjectives by relating them to their opposites (antonyms). c. Identify real-life connections between words and their use (e.g., note places at school that are colorful). d. Distinguish shades of meaning among verbs describing the same general action (e.g., *walk, march, strut, prance*) by acting out the meanings.
	K **L.K.6:** Use words and phrases acquired through conversations, reading and being read to, and responding to texts.
	1 **L.1.4:** Determine or clarify the meaning of unknown and multiple-meaning words and phrases based on grade 1 reading and content, choosing flexibly from an array of strategies. a. Use sentence-level context as a clue to the meaning of a word or phrase. b. Use frequently occurring affixes as a clue to the meaning of a word. c. Identify frequently occurring root words (e.g., *look*) and their inflectional forms (e.g., *looks, looked, looking*).
	1 **L.1.5:** With guidance and support from adults, demonstrate understanding of word relationships and nuances in word meanings. a. Sort words into categories (e.g., colors, clothing) to gain a sense of the concepts the categories represent. b. Define words by category and by one or more key attributes (e.g., *a duck is a bird that swims; a tiger is a large cat with stripes*). c. Identify real-life connections between words and their use (e.g., note places at home that are cozy).

continued

continued from previous

Speaking and Listening Standards	Language Standards
	d. Distinguish shades of meaning among verbs differing in manner (e.g., *look, peek, glance, stare, glare, scowl*) and adjectives differing in intensity (e.g., *large, gigantic*) by defining or choosing them or by acting out the meanings.
	1 **L.1.6:** Use words and phrases acquired through conversations, reading and being read to, and responding to texts, including using frequently occurring conjunctions to signal simple relationships (e.g., *because*).
2 **SL.2.3:** Ask and answer questions about what a speaker says in order to clarify comprehension, gather additional information, or deepen understanding of a topic or issue.	**2** **L.2.3:** Use knowledge of language and its conventions when writing, speaking, reading, or listening. a. Compare formal and informal uses of English.
	2 **L.2.4:** Determine or clarify the meaning of unknown and multiple-meaning words and phrases based on grade 2 reading and content, choosing flexibly from an array of strategies. a. Use sentence-level context as a clue to the meaning of a word or phrase. b. Determine the meaning of the new word formed when a known prefix is added to a known word (e.g., *happy/unhappy, tell/retell*). c. Use a known root word as a clue to the meaning of an unknown word with the same root (e.g., *addition, additional*). d. Use knowledge of the meaning of individual words to predict the meaning of compound words (e.g., *birdhouse, lighthouse, housefly; bookshelf, notebook, bookmark*). e. Use glossaries and beginning dictionaries, both print and digital, to determine or clarify the meaning of words and phrases in all content areas.
	2 **L.2.5:** Demonstrate understanding of word relationships and nuances in word meanings. a. Identify real-life connections between words and their use (e.g., describe foods that are spicy or juicy). b. Distinguish shades of meaning among closely related verbs (e.g., *toss, throw, hurl*) and closely related adjectives (e.g., *thin, slender, skinny, scrawny*).
	2 **L.2.6:** Use words and phrases acquired through conversations, reading and being read to, and responding to texts, including using adjectives and adverbs to describe (e.g., *When other kids are happy that makes me happy*).

In addition to the CCSS ELA Language and Speaking Listening standards listed in the chart, ELD Standard 8 Analyzing language choices is **also** correlated with ELA Reading Literature standards K.4–5, 1.4–5, and 2.4–5, and Reading Information standards K.4, 1.4, and 2.4–5.

Source: *Common Core State Standards, K–12 English Language Arts* (2010).

What the **Teacher** Does

Word conscious environments are those in which children and adults notice and discuss words. Children may create word walls, word jars, or word journals in which they record words that are important, fascinating, or that otherwise capture their attention. They talk about words in different contexts, and notice relationships among words and similarities among words in different languages. They think about author's choices and their own choices. Their awareness of words is heightened (p. 206).

Teachers can assist students with distinguishing how two different frequently used words produce a different effect, by

- Engaging students in a language study, where they highlight key vocabulary and/or grammar that were used by the author. The teacher can chart these words on a poster so that students can make the same or different language choices when they write their own stories or essays.

- Having students discuss how different language choices impacted them as readers and/or listeners. They can identify those key words and create a word bank, so that they can use theme in their own writing.

- Showing students two paragraphs written on the same topic, but with different language emphasized, and compare how it impacts meaning.

- Having students revise their own writing, by providing a word bank, in order to produce a different effect.

- Posting a familiar text selection on the board, and asking students to revise the paragraph by using a word bank of words that have been explicitly taught.

Tips for Differentiation by Proficiency Level

- *Emerging*—At the emerging stage, the teacher can use sentence strips with familiar text and replace key vocabulary in a sentence, in order to demonstrate for students how language choices can impact meaning.

- *Expanding*—At the expanding stage, students can work with sentence strips in pairs to analyze and change language of a familiar text.

- *Bridging*—At the bridging level, students can work with each other to highlight key words in their own writing (or a cloze passage), and begin to replace them with words that may have stronger meaning.

Source: 2014 ELA/ELD Framework, p. 206.

Notes

Academic Vocabulary—Key Words and Phrases Related to Standard 8: Analyzing language choices

Adjectives: Words that describe or modify a person or thing in a sentence. Adjectives are used to describe nouns.

Distinguish shades of meaning: This refers to nuances in words with similar meanings, such as *weep* versus *cry*. Weeping may be quiet sobbing, while crying suggests loud sobbing.

Frequently occurring verbs and adjectives: These are words that come up often in texts that students read. They are good words to focus on with students, because they are so familiar, in order to build word webs or understand opposites.

Language choices: Choosing to use formal or informal English depending on the purpose of the conversation, the task at hand, and the audience. Choices include use of vocabulary, use of dialogue, inclusion of idioms and slang, need for academic language, etc.

Nuances in word meanings: The subtle meaning of words that help students choose one word over another in order to convey a specific meaning.

Sufficiency of evidence: Determining if the author has provided enough evidence to support the main idea of the text.

Verbs: Words that name actions or states of being; they change form to indicate tense, number, voice, or mood. Students will be able to tell the difference between thinking and feeling verbs and doing and having verbs as they learn to analyze language choices by authors.

Word walls or jars: Any kind of open repository for saving important words that students will want to refer to and use in their speaking and writing.

Source: Taberski & Burke, (2014), *The Common Core Companion: The Standards Decoded, Grades K–2.*

Notes

Example of Practice in Snapshot Related to Standard 8: Analyzing language choices

Vignette 4.2. Discussing " Doing" Verbs in *Chrysanthemum* Designated ELD Instruction in Grade 2

Mrs. Hernandez explains that there are still a lot of thinking/feeling and being/having verbs in a story, and there are many *saying* verbs because there is a lot of dialogue in stories, but that today, they are mostly focusing on the doing verbs that show what a character is feeling or thinking. She tells them that they may also find examples of saying verbs that do this. For example, an author may write, *"she sighed,"* to show that a character is disappointed or sad.

She writes this on the chart as an example. Mrs. Hernandez tells the children that their next task is to be *language detectives*. She has the students work in groups of three to find other examples in books by Kevin Henkes where he shows how a character is feeling or is thinking by using doing or saying verbs. She gives the triads copies of several Kevin Henkes books, along with a graphic organizer like the one she used to model the task. For each book, some examples have been written in the left-hand column and a space in the right-hand column is for students to write their *translations*.

She tells the students that their task is to find a sentence in the text that they think uses doing verbs to show what a character feels or what a character thinks. Next, the groups of three try to agree on what they will write and record it on the graphic organizer, discussing why the author used the doing verb instead of a being/having or thinking/feeling verb with an adjective. As the students engage in the task, she observes their discussions and provides just-in-time scaffolding when needed. Once the time for the task is up, she calls the students back to the rug to discuss their findings. Mrs. Hernandez asks students to tell her where to place the verbs on the Verb Chart, which she posts in the room, along with the Using Verbs to Show and Tell chart, so that children will have models for their own story writing.

Primary CA ELD Standards Addressed (Expanding):

ELD.PI.2.1—Contribute to class, group, and partner discussions . . . ; ELD.PI.2.6— Describe ideas, phenomena (e.g., how earthworms eat), and text elements (e.g., setting, events) in greater detail based on understanding of a variety of grade-level texts and viewing of multimedia with moderate support; ELD.PII.2.3—Use a growing number of verb types (e.g., doing, saying, being/having, thinking/feeling) with increasing independence.

The snapshots and vignettes cited above can be found in their entirety at https://www.cde.ca.gov/ci/rl/cf/, *ELA/ELD Framework*, pp. 346–347.

Part 1

INTERACTING IN MEANINGFUL WAYS

C *Productive Mode*

Introduction

Part I of the *California ELD Standards* promotes English Language Learners' abilities to *interact in meaningful ways* so that they acquire English and develop content knowledge simultaneously. Part I **comes first in the standards** to emphasize that students need to interact with adults and each other about meaning and content before they enter deeply into how the English language works. Part I, Interacting in Meaningful Ways, is subdivided into three clusters of standards that emphasize student participation in the major modes of communication: Collaborative, Interpretive, and Productive.

Cluster C: Productive Mode Standards have the same general descriptions K–12 for the four standards in the cluster, related to the creation of oral presentations and written texts. These include

1. *Expressing Information and ideas in formal oral presentations on academic topics.* Beyond collaborating and interpreting language, students need multiple opportunities to produce what they are learning for college, career, and civic life. These include rich language experiences, word-learning strategies, fostering word consciousness, and language play (Graves, 2000, 2006, 2009). Students are able to produce meaningful oral presentations that communicate their thinking on what they are learning.

2. *Composing/writing literary and informational texts to present, describe, and explain ideas and information, using appropriate technology.* Knowing how to make appropriate language choices will enable students to produce their own written texts (such as narratives, explanation, and arguments) (Brisk, 2012; Schleppegrell & de Oliveira, 2006).

3. *Supporting own opinions and evaluating others' opinions in speaking and writing.* This skill enables students to find and use text evidence in constructing their own opinions and also evaluating the opinions of others (Dutro & Kinsella, 2010; Gersten et al., 2007).

4. *Selecting and applying varied and precise vocabulary and language structures to effectively convey ideas.* In the CA ELD standards, English is considered a meaning-making resource, one which uses text structure, grammatical structures, and vocabulary as part of making meaning (Bailey & Huang 2011; Wong Fillmore & Fillmore, 2012). Vocabulary knowledge is a powerful factor in making meaning, both domain-specific and general academic vocabulary (Calderon et al., 2005; Spycher, 2009; Townsend & Collins, 2009).

In *The California ELD Companion*, the What the Student Does section provides specific descriptions of competence with each of the Productive standards at the appropriate grade range and proficiency level. Similarly, the What the Teacher Does section provides specific strategies for developing competence with each of the Productive standards at the appropriate grade range. And the last section, Vignettes and Snapshots, offers classroom-level descriptions of what each standard looks like in practice.

Source: *California English Language Development Standards, K–12* (2012). Chapter 4, "Theoretical Foundations and the Research Bases of the CA ELD Standards," provides an excellent summary of the research used in developing the four Productive standards in Part I, C.

Emerging

K Plan and deliver very brief oral presentations (e.g., show and tell, describing a picture).

1 Plan and deliver very brief oral presentations (e.g., show and tell, describing a picture).

2 Plan and deliver very brief oral presentations (e.g., recounting an experience, retelling a story, describing a picture).

Expanding

K Plan and deliver brief oral presentations *on a variety of topics* (e.g., show and tell, *author's chair, recounting an experience, describing an animal*).

1 Plan and deliver brief oral presentations *on a variety of topics* (e.g., show and tell, *author's chair, recounting an experience, describing an animal, and the like*).

2 Plan and deliver *brief oral presentations on a variety of topics* (e.g., *retelling a story, describing an animal*).

Bridging

K Plan and deliver *longer* oral presentations on a variety of topics *in a variety of content areas* (e.g., *retelling a story, describing a science experiment*).

1 Plan and deliver *longer* oral presentations on a variety of topics in a *variety of content areas* (e.g., *retelling a story, describing a science experiment*).

2 Plan and deliver *longer* oral presentations on a variety of topics and *content areas* (e.g., retelling a story, *recounting a science experiment, describing how to solve a mathematics problem*).

Script *in bold italics* indicates content not found in earlier proficiency levels of the same ELD Standard.

Source: *California English Language Development Standards for Grades K–12*, California Department of Education (2012).

Notes

What the **Student** Does

Emerging	Expanding	Bridging

Gist: Students can plan and deliver brief oral presentations on a variety of topics.

Emerging	Expanding	Bridging
K **They consider:** • What am I trying to say? • Am I using complete sentences? • For show and tell, am I listening to the other students' questions about my item?	**K** **They *also* consider:** • Do I use the right verbs to tell about something happening now or in the past?	**K** **They *also* consider:** • Do I include adjectives with my description to make the presentation clearer? • In telling about a science experiment, do I organize my presentation by the steps in the process?

Gist: Students can plan and deliver brief oral presentations on a variety of topics in a variety of content areas.

Emerging	Expanding	Bridging
1 **They consider:** • What am I trying to say or express? • Am I using complete sentences? • For retelling a story, am I using temporal words (*first, next, then*) to help my listeners understand?	**1** **They *also* consider:** • Do I use the right verbs to tell about something happening now or in the past? • For author's chair, am I listening to what the other students are saying about my writing?	**1** **They *also* consider:** • Do I include adjectives with my description to make the presentation clearer? • In telling about a science experiment, do I organize my presentation by the steps in the process?

Gist: Students can plan and deliver longer oral presentations on a variety of topics in a variety of content areas.

Emerging	Expanding	Bridging
2 **They consider:** • What am I trying to say or express? • Am I using complete sentences? • For retelling a story, am I using temporal words (*first, next, then*) to help my listeners understand?	**2** **They *also* consider:** • Do I use the right verbs to tell about something happening now or in the past? • Do I include adjectives with my description to make the presentation clearer?	**2** **They *also* consider:** • What facts and details should I add to help describe or explain my story? • In telling about a science experiment or math problem, do I organize my presentation by the steps in the process?

Source: California English Language Development Standards for Grades K–12 (2012).

Speaking and Listening Standards	**Language Standards**
K **SL.K.4:** Describe familiar people, places, things, and events and, with prompting and support, provide additional detail.	**K** **L.K.1:** Demonstrate command of the conventions of standard English grammar and usage when writing or speaking. a. Print many upper- and lowercase letters. b. Use frequently occurring nouns and verbs. c. Form regular plural nouns orally by adding /s/ or /es/ (e.g., *dog, dogs; wish, wishes*). d. Understand and use question words (interrogatives) (e.g., *who, what, where, when, why, how*). e. Use the most frequently occurring prepositions (e.g., *to, from, in, out, on, off, for, of, by, with*). f. Produce and expand complete sentences in shared language activities.
K **SL.K.5:** Add drawings or other visual displays to descriptions as desired to provide additional detail.	**K** **L.K.6:** Use words and phrases acquired through conversations, reading and being read to, and responding to texts.
K **SL.K.6:** Speak audibly and express thoughts, feelings, and ideas clearly.	
1 **SL.1.4:** Describe people, places, things, and events with relevant details, expressing ideas and feelings clearly. a. Memorize and recite poems, rhymes, and songs with expression.	**1** **L.1.1:** Demonstrate command of the conventions of standard English grammar and usage when writing or speaking. a. Print all upper- and lowercase letters. b. Use common, proper, and possessive nouns. c. Use singular and plural nouns with matching verbs in basic sentences (e.g., *He hops; We hop*). d. Use personal (subject, object), possessive, and indefinite pronouns (e.g., *I, me, my; they, them, their; anyone, everything*). e. Use verbs to convey a sense of past, present, and future (e.g., *Yesterday I walked home; Today I walk home; Tomorrow I will walk home*). f. Use frequently occurring adjectives. g. Use frequently occurring conjunctions (e.g., *and, but, or, so, because*). h. Use determiners (e.g., articles, demonstratives). i. Use frequently occurring prepositions (e.g., *during, beyond, toward*). j. Produce and expand complete simple and compound declarative, interrogative, imperative, and exclamatory sentences in response to prompts.

continued

continued from previous

Speaking and Listening Standards	Language Standards
1 **SL.1.5:** Add drawings or other visual displays to descriptions when appropriate to clarify ideas, thoughts, and feelings.	**1** **L.1.6:** Use words and phrases acquired through conversations, reading and being read to, and responding to texts, including using frequently occurring conjunctions to signal simple relationships (e.g., *because*).
1 **SL.1.6:** Produce complete sentences when appropriate to task and situation. (See grade 1 Language standards 1 and 3 for specific expectations.)	
2 **SL.2.4:** Tell a story or recount an experience with appropriate facts and relevant, descriptive details, speaking audibly in coherent sentences. a. Plan and deliver a narrative presentation that: recounts a well-elaborated event, includes details, reflects a logical sequence, and provides a conclusion.	**2** **L.2.1:** Demonstrate command of the conventions of standard English grammar and usage when writing or speaking. a. Use collective nouns (e.g., *group*). b. Form and use frequently occurring irregular plural nouns (e.g., *feet, children, teeth, mice, fish*). c. Use reflexive pronouns (e.g., *myself, ourselves*). d. Form and use the past tense of frequently occurring irregular verbs (e.g., *sat, hid, told*). e. Use adjectives and adverbs, and choose between them depending on what is to be modified. f. Produce, expand, and rearrange complete simple and compound sentences (e.g., *The boy watched the movie; The little boy watched the movie; The action movie was watched by the little boy*). g. Create readable documents with legible print.
2 **SL.2.5:** Create audio recordings of stories or poems; add drawings or other visual displays to stories or recounts of experiences when appropriate to clarify ideas, thoughts, and feelings.	**2** **L.2.3:** Use knowledge of language and its conventions when writing, speaking, reading, or listening. a. Compare formal and informal uses of English.
2 **SL.2.6:** Produce complete sentences when appropriate to task and situation in order to provide requested detail or clarification. (See grade 2 Language standards 1 and 3 for specific expectations.)	**2** **L.2.6:** Use words and phrases acquired through conversations, reading and being read to, and responding to texts, including using adjectives and adverbs to describe (e.g., *When other kids are happy that makes me happy*).

Source: *Common Core State Standards, K–12 English Language Arts* (2010).

What the **Teacher** Does

Teachers ensure that students have adequate background knowledge and vocabulary to present ideas and information effectively. They provide instruction and demonstrate effective presentations themselves, and they debrief with children, as appropriate. Presenting in Grade 1 takes many forms:

- Retelling a familiar story
- Explaining how to perform a task
- Sharing with others a group experience
- "Reading" a wordless picture book
- Reporting the outcome of a research project
- Reciting, with expression, poems and rhymes that have been memorized (SL.1.4a)
- Singing, with expression, songs that have been memorized (SL.1.4a) (p. 245)

Teachers can assist students with planning and delivering longer oral presentations:

- Having students use familiar pictures or realia from home to make detailed presentations.
- Having students present the beginning, middle, and end of a story using picture walks. Students can be provided with transition words such as first, next, last.
- Providing models of effective student oral presentations from the Teaching Channel or previous classes. After viewing the video, discuss with students the effective elements that were included, as well as next steps.
- Creating and providing students with a rubric that lists the effective elements of an effective presentation, depending on the expectations for the presentation. Have students use the rubric as they develop an oral presentation. Teachers can us rubistar.4teachers.org to create their rubrics.
- Having students jointly construct a presentation and practice presenting to each other. Students can provide feedback on each other's segments by using the rubric previously introduced.
- Having students use their phones to digitally record each other while presenting, and then provide feedback using the rubric previously shared.

Tips for Differentiation by Proficiency Level

- *Emerging*—At the emerging level, students can use a Think-Pair-Share with a sentence frame to retell the beginning, middle, and end of a story. The sentence frame can include, *"At the beginning of the story _____," "In the middle of the story, _____,"* and *"Finally, at the end of the story, _____."*

- *Expanding*—At the expanding level, the Think-Pair-Share can be focused on the language that students used to retell. This can include, *"I used _____ verbs and _____ adjectives to retell my story because _____."*

- *Bridging*—At the bridging level, students' Think-Pair-Shares can be focused on retelling the steps in the process used in math or science. For example, *"I used the following steps, _____, to answer the math problem because _____."*

Source: 2014 ELA/ELD Framework, p. 245.

Academic Vocabulary—Key Words and Phrases Related to Standard 9: Presenting

Author's chair: A special time and place for writers who wish to share their final products with an audience. Because the writing has already gone through revising and editing based on constructive criticism, Author's Chair is an opportunity for the writers to receive positive feedback from their classmates.

Oral presentation: Explaining something to an audience for the purpose of informing, entertaining, or persuading. Depending on the topic and the audience, oral presentations may use informal or formal English, but in all cases, should be thoughtfully prepared by the speaker to convey meaning.

Recounting a story: Using the teller's own words to summarize a story that is familiar. Recounting usually involves a description of character, setting, plot or problem, and solution. Recounting does not include analysis of the story itself.

Show and tell: Often the first oral presentations that young students are asked to do, telling something about a familiar object from home. Simple sentence frames, such as *"I have a _____," "I got it from_____,"* or *"I like it because_____,"* help early speakers to ease into what they want to say.

Think-Pair-Share: Using a collaborative strategy that requires students to (1) think individually about a topic or answer to a question and (2) share ideas with classmates.

Source: Taberski & Burke, (2014), *The Common Core Companion: The Standards Decoded, Grades K–2.*

Notes

Example of Practice in Snapshot Related to Standard 9: Presenting

Vignette 3.2. Retelling *The Three Little Pigs* Using Past Tense Verbs and Expanded Sentences—Designated ELD Instruction in Transitional Kindergarten

Ms. Campbell invites the six EL children at the Emerging level of English language proficiency over to the teaching table. She tells them that today, they are going to retell the story of *The Three Little Pigs* again, but that this time, they are going to focus on adding a lot of details to their retellings and making sure listeners know that the events in the story took place in the past. She points to the story map that the class generated the previous week.

Ms. Campbell places the same five pictures the students have already used for orally retelling the story in ELA (see Vignette 3.1) on the table in front of them. She hands each of the six children a popsicle stick puppet (three pigs and three wolves). She explains that when there is dialogue, they will each have a chance to act out how the character is saying the dialogue using the puppets.

CA ELD Standards Addressed (Emerging): ELD.PI.K.12a—Retell texts and recount experiences using complete sentences and key words; ELD.PII.K.3b—Use simple verb tenses appropriate for the text type and discipline to convey time . . . ; ELD.PII.K.4— Expand noun phrases in simple ways (e.g., adding a familiar adjective to describe a noun) . . . ; ELD.PII.K.5—Expand sentences with frequently used prepositional phrases (e.g., in the house, on the boat) to provide details (e.g., time, manner, place, cause) . . .

The snapshots and vignettes cited above can be found in their entirety at https://www.cde.ca.gov/ci/rl/cf/, *ELA/ELD Framework*, p. 197.

Notes

Notes

Emerging

K Draw, dictate, and write to compose very short literary texts (e.g., story) and informational texts (e.g., a description of a dog), using familiar vocabulary collaboratively in shared language activities with an adult (e.g., joint construction of texts), with peers, and sometimes independently.

1 Write very short literary texts (e.g., story) and informational texts (e.g., a description of an insect) using familiar vocabulary collaboratively with an adult (e.g., joint construction of texts), with peers, and sometimes independently.

2 Write very short literary texts (e.g., story) and informational texts (e.g., a description of a volcano) using familiar vocabulary collaboratively with an adult (e.g., joint construction of texts), with peers, and sometimes independently.

Expanding

K Draw, dictate, and write to compose short literary texts (e.g., story) and informational texts (e.g., a description of dogs), collaboratively with an adult (e.g., joint construction of texts), with peers, and *with increasing independence*.

1 Write *short literary texts* (e.g., a story) and informational texts *(e.g., an informative text on the life cycle of an insect)* collaboratively with an adult (e.g., joint construction of texts), with peers, and *with increasing independence*.

2 Write *short literary texts* (e.g., a story) and informational texts *(e.g., an explanatory text explaining how a volcano erupts)* collaboratively with an adult (e.g., joint construction of texts), with peers, and *with increasing independence*.

Bridging

K Draw, dictate, and write to compose *longer literary texts* (e.g., story) and informational texts *(e.g., an information report on dogs)*, collaboratively with an adult (e.g., joint construction of texts), with peers, *and independently using appropriate text organization*.

1 Write *longer literary texts* (e.g., a story) and informational texts (e.g., an informative text on the life cycle of insects) collaboratively with an adult (e.g., joint construction), with peers, and *independently*.

2 Write *longer literary texts* (e.g., a story) and informational texts (e.g., an explanatory text explaining how a volcano erupts) collaboratively with an adult (e.g., joint construction), with peers and *independently*.

Script *in bold italics* indicates content not found in earlier proficiency levels of the same ELD Standard.

Source: *California English Language Development Standards for Grades K–12,* California Department of Education (2012).

What the **Student** Does

Emerging	Expanding	Bridging
Gist: *Students can draw, dictate, and write short literary texts and informational texts collaboratively with an adult and with peers.*		
K They consider: • What picture can I draw to show my idea? • What do I think about this topic or book?	**K** They *also* consider: • What picture can I draw to go with my words?	**K** They *also* consider: • What do I want to explain about this topic or book? • What is my part in this joint writing assignment?
Gist: *Students can write short literary texts and informational texts collaboratively with an adult, with peers, and sometimes independently.*		
1 They consider: • What do I think about this topic or book? • What picture can I draw to go with my words?	**1** They *also* consider: • What facts or details do I want to include? • What is my part in this joint writing assignment?	**1** They *also* consider: • When I reread my text, does it make sense to me? Will others understand it?
Gist: : *Students can write literary texts and informational texts collaboratively with an adult, with peers, and independently.*		
2 They consider: • Am I clear about my topic? Is it too broad or too narrow? • What is my part in this joint writing assignment?	**2** They *also* consider: • What facts or details do I want to include? • When I reread my text, does it make sense to me? Will others understand it?	**2** They *also* consider: • What should I say first, second, and third to make my topic clear to everyone? • What do I want to say as a final point or ending?

Speaking and Listening Standards	Language Standards
	K **L.K.1:** Demonstrate command of the conventions of standard English grammar and usage when writing or speaking. a. Print many upper- and lowercase letters. b. Use frequently occurring nouns and verbs. c. Form regular plural nouns orally by adding /s/ or /es/ (e.g., *dog, dogs; wish, wishes*). d. Understand and use question words (interrogatives) (e.g., *who, what, where, when, why, how*). e. Use the most frequently occurring prepositions (e.g., *to, from, in, out, on, off, for, of, by, with*). f. Produce and expand complete sentences in shared language activities.
	K **L.K.2:** Demonstrate command of the conventions of standard English capitalization, punctuation, and spelling when writing. a. Capitalize the first word in a sentence and the pronoun I. b. Recognize and name end punctuation. c. Write a letter or letters for most consonant and short-vowel sounds (phonemes). d. Spell simple words phonetically, drawing on knowledge of sound-letter relationships.
	K **L.K.6:** Use words and phrases acquired through conversations, reading and being read to, and responding to texts.
	1 **L.1.1:** Demonstrate command of the conventions of standard English grammar and usage when writing or speaking. a. Print all upper- and lowercase letters. b. Use common, proper, and possessive nouns. c. Use singular and plural nouns with matching verbs in basic sentences (e.g., *He hops; We hop*). d. Use personal (subject, object), possessive, and indefinite pronouns (e.g., *I, me, my; they, them, their; anyone, everything*). e. Use verbs to convey a sense of past, present, and future (e.g., *Yesterday I walked home; Today I walk home; Tomorrow I will walk home*). f. Use frequently occurring adjectives.

continued

continued from previous

Speaking and Listening Standards	Language Standards
	g. Use frequently occurring conjunctions (e.g., *and, but, or, so, because*).
	h. Use determiners (e.g., articles, demonstratives).
	i. Use frequently occurring prepositions (e.g., *during, beyond, toward*).
	j. Produce and expand complete simple and compound declarative, interrogative, imperative, and exclamatory sentences in response to prompts.
	1 **L.1.2:** Demonstrate command of the conventions of standard English capitalization, punctuation, and spelling when writing.
	a. Capitalize dates and names of people.
	b. Use end punctuation for sentences.
	c. Use commas in dates and to separate single words in a series.
	d. Use conventional spelling for words with common spelling patterns and for frequently occurring irregular words.
	e. Spell untaught words phonetically, drawing on phonemic awareness and spelling conventions.
	1 **L.1.6:** Use words and phrases acquired through conversations, reading and being read to, and responding to texts, including using frequently occurring conjunctions to signal simple relationships (e.g., *because*).
	2 **L.2.1:** Demonstrate command of the conventions of standard English grammar and usage when writing or speaking.
	a. Use collective nouns (e.g., *group*).
	b. Form and use frequently occurring irregular plural nouns (e.g., *feet, children, teeth, mice, fish*).
	c. Use reflexive pronouns (e.g., *myself, ourselves*).
	d. Form and use the past tense of frequently occurring irregular verbs (e.g., *sat, hid, told*).
	e. Use adjectives and adverbs and choose between them depending on what is to be modified.
	f. Produce, expand, and rearrange complete simple and compound sentences (e.g., *The boy watched the movie; The little boy watched the movie; The action movie was watched by the little boy*).
	g. Create readable documents with legible print.

continued from previous

Speaking and Listening Standards	Language Standards
	2 **L.2.2:** Demonstrate command of the conventions of standard English capitalization, punctuation, and spelling when writing. a. Capitalize holidays, product names, and geographic names. b. Use commas in greetings and closings of letters. c. Use an apostrophe to form contractions and frequently occurring possessives. d. Generalize learned spelling patterns when writing words (e.g., *cage—badge; boy—boil*). e. Consult reference materials, including beginning dictionaries, as needed to check and correct spellings.
	2 **L.2.3:** Use knowledge of language and its conventions when writing, speaking, reading, or listening. a. Compare formal and informal uses of English.
	2 **L.2.6:** Use words and phrases acquired through conversations, reading and being read to, and responding to texts, including using adjectives and adverbs to describe (e.g., *When other kids are happy that makes me happy*).

In addition to the ELA Language standards provided in this chart, ELD Standard 10: Composing/Writing is **also** correlated with ELA Writing standards K.1–3, 5–8, 1.1–3, 5–8, 2.1–8, and 2.10.

Source: *Common Core State Standards, K–12 English Language Arts* (2010).

Notes

What the **Teacher** Does

Children's emerging writing abilities are exciting to observe. These abilities develop within a writing-rich environment with instruction that carefully guides and supports children as they learn to write. Children learn to write as their teachers share excellent examples of writing, model writing themselves, provide numerous opportunities for children to respond in writing to texts and learning experiences across content areas, and provide explicit instruction (p. 207).

Teachers can assist students with writing very short literary texts (e.g., story) and informational texts (e.g., a description of a volcano) using familiar vocabulary collaboratively with an adult (e.g., joint construction of texts), with peers, and sometimes independently:

- Providing students with picture prompts from familiar texts where they can write about the story or rewrite the story.

- Modeling the writing process for students by jointly constructing a composition about a text that has been read as a class. The teacher can begin the composition on the board, and then have students complete the piece on their own using sentence frames and word banks.

- Having two students jointly compose a writing piece together about a familiar topic using both sentence frames to begin responses and a word bank with key words.

- Using academic oral language as a scaffold for the writing process (see Example of Practice Snapshot 3.11). Teachers can use classroom conversations as starting points for the writing process by using sentence frames what will mirror the language and content that students will write about. When teachers use sentence frames for writing, they can model syntactically and grammatically correct writing forms. When students use sentence frames for writing, they can focus their attention instead on the content and can internalize the language structure of the sentence frame.

Tips for Differentiation by Proficiency Level

- *Emerging* —At the emerging level, students can begin writing about familiar topics, such as their interests or their opinions about topics. A sentence frame that can be used for this is "*I think this book [or topic] _____.*"

- *Expanding* —At the expanding level, students can begin to provide more information about a text, and can use the frame "*I think this book [or topic] _____ because _____.*"

- *Bridging* —At the bridging level, students can complete longer selections and can expand upon their ideas. Student can begin to use transition words in their writing such as, first, second, and lastly.

Source: 2014 ELA/ELD Framework, p. 207.

Academic Vocabulary—Key Words and Phrases Related to Standard 10: Composing/writing

Informational texts: Texts written to give information or explanation about a topic, including descriptions, procedures, recount or retells, information reports, explanations, expositions, and analyses.

Joint construction of texts: Working together to design a piece of writing, taking responsibility for individual parts, offering responses to each other's writing, and combining all the parts into one cohesive text.

Literary texts: Including stories (fantasy, legends, fables), drama, poetry, retellings

Purpose of persuading: The speaker or writer is seeking to influence the thinking of the listener or reader to be in agreement with the speaker or writer. Examples include first person essays, a literary response, debates, or op-ed pieces in the newspaper. Formal English is more often used for the purpose of persuading.

Sentence frames: If students are struggling to find the right words to explain, describe, and clarify what they are thinking, a sentence starter or sentence frame helps them to get the idea started. For example, *"I think the statement is true because_____,"* or *"This makes me wonder_____."* Sentence frames can be open ended or closed.

Source: Taberski & Burke, (2014), *The Common Core Companion: The Standards Decoded, Grades K–2.*

Notes

Example of Practice in Snapshot Related to Standard 10: Composing/writing

Snapshot 3.11. Expanding Sentences and Building Vocabulary Designated ELD Connected to ELA/Social Studies in Grade 1

[In Social Studies], Mr. Dupont takes care to emphasize American and international heroes that reflect his students' diverse backgrounds. He frequently asks the children to discuss their ideas and opinions in order to prepare them to write an opinion piece explaining why they admire a historical figure mentioned in one of the texts they have been reading.

Because Mr. Dupont's EL children are at the Bridging level of English language proficiency, during designated ELD, he provides his students with extended opportunities to discuss their ideas and opinions, as he knows that this will support them later when writing down their ideas. He strategically targets particular language that he would like students to use in their opinion pieces by constructing sentence frames that contain specific vocabulary and grammatical structures that will enable his students to be more precise and detailed (e.g., "*My favorite hero is* _____ *because* _____. _____ *was* very courageous *when* _____."). He explains to the children how they can expand their ideas in different ways by adding information about where, when, how, and so forth. For example, he explains that instead of simply saying, "She worked on a farm," children could say, "She worked on a farm *in California*," or they could add even more detail and precision by saying, "She worked on a farm *in the central valley of California*." He provides his students with many opportunities to construct these expanded sentence structures as the students discuss the historical figures they are learning about and then write short summaries of their discussions at the end of each lesson. During these lessons, he encourages the children to refer to the texts they have previously read together and to cite evidence from them to support their ideas.

CA ELD Standards (Bridging): ELD.PI.K–1.1, 3, 6, 10, 12b; ELD.PII.K–1.4–5, 6

CA CCSS for ELA/Literacy: RI.1.1; SL.1.1, 4, 6; L.1.6

The snapshots and vignettes cited above can be found in their entirety at https://www.cde.ca.gov/ci/rl/cf/, *ELA/ELD Framework*, p. 260.

Notes

Emerging

K   Offer opinions and provide good reasons (e.g., *My favorite book is X because X.*) referring to the text or to relevant background knowledge.

1   Offer opinions and provide good reasons (e.g., *My favorite book is X because X*) referring to the text or to relevant background knowledge.

2   Support opinions by providing good reasons and some textual evidence or relevant background knowledge (e.g., referring to textual evidence or knowledge of content).

Expanding

K   Offer opinions and provide good reasons and *some textual evidence* or relevant background knowledge (*e.g., paraphrased examples from text or knowledge of content*).

1   Offer opinions and provide good reasons and *some textual evidence* or relevant background knowledge (*e.g., paraphrased examples from text or knowledge of content*).

2   Support opinions by providing good reasons and *increasingly detailed textual evidence (e.g., providing examples from the text)* or relevant background knowledge about the content.

Bridging

K   Offer opinions and provide good reasons with *detailed textual evidence* or relevant background knowledge (*e.g., specific examples from text or knowledge of content*).

1   Offer opinions and provide good reasons with *detailed textual evidence* or relevant background knowledge (*e.g., specific examples from text or knowledge of content*).

2   Support opinions or *persuade others* by providing good reasons and detailed textual evidence (*e.g., specific events or graphics from text*) or relevant background knowledge about the content.

Script *in bold italics* indicates content not found in earlier proficiency levels of the same ELD Standard.

Source: *California English Language Development Standards for Grades K–12*, California Department of Education (2012).

Notes

What the **Student** Does

Emerging	Expanding	Bridging
Gist: *Students can offer opinions and provide good reasons with some text evidence or background knowledge.*		
K They consider: • What do I think about this topic? • Why do I think this? What tells me so or persuades me?	**K** They *also* consider: • What do I already know that helps me form my opinion about this topic? • Do I have examples from the text that support my opinion?	**K** Same as Expanding.
Gist: *Students can offer opinions and provide good reasons with specific text evidence or background knowledge.*		
1 They consider: • What do I think about this topic? • Why do I think this? What tells me so or persuades me?	**1** They *also* consider: • What do I already know that helps me form my opinion about this topic? • Do I have examples from the text that support my opinion?	**1** Same as Expanding.
Gist: *Students can support opinions or persuade others by providing good reasons with detailed text evidence or background knowledge.*		
2 They consider: • I know what I think, but can I support my opinion? • What do I already know that helps me form my opinion about this topic? • Do I have examples from the text that support my opinion?	**2** They *also* consider: • What facts or details do I want to include to support my opinion?	**2** They *also* consider: • Does my opinion seem persuasive? Can I back it up with detailed evidence and background knowledge?

Source: *California English Language Development Standards for Grades K–12* (2012).

Speaking and Listening Standards	Language Standards
K **SL.K.4:** Describe familiar people, places, things, and events and, with prompting and support, provide additional detail.	K **L.K.1:** Demonstrate command of the conventions of standard English grammar and usage when writing or speaking. a. Print many upper- and lowercase letters. b. Use frequently occurring nouns and verbs. c. Form regular plural nouns orally by adding /s/ or /es/ (e.g., *dog, dogs; wish, wishes*). d. Understand and use question words (interrogatives) (e.g., *who, what, where, when, why, how*). e. Use the most frequently occurring prepositions (e.g., *to, from, in, out, on, off, for, of, by, with*). f. Produce and expand complete sentences in shared language activities.
K **SL.K.6:** Speak audibly and express thoughts, feelings, and ideas clearly.	K **L.K.2:** Demonstrate command of the conventions of standard English capitalization, punctuation, and spelling when writing. a. Capitalize the first word in a sentence and the pronoun *I*. b. Recognize and name end punctuation. c. Write a letter or letters for most consonant and short-vowel sounds (phonemes). d. Spell simple words phonetically, drawing on knowledge of sound–letter relationships.
	K **L.K.6:** Use words and phrases acquired through conversations, reading and being read to, and responding to texts.
1 **SL.1.4:** Describe people, places, things, and events with relevant details, expressing ideas and feelings clearly. a. Memorize and recite poems, rhymes, and songs with expression.	1 **L.1.1:** Demonstrate command of the conventions of standard English grammar and usage when writing or speaking. a. Print all upper- and lowercase letters. b. Use common, proper, and possessive nouns. c. Use singular and plural nouns with matching verbs in basic sentences (e.g., *He hops; We hop*). d. Use personal (subject, object), possessive, and indefinite pronouns (e.g., *I, me, my; they, them, their; anyone, everything*). e. Use verbs to convey a sense of past, present, and future (e.g., *Yesterday I walked home; Today I walk home; Tomorrow I will walk home*). f. Use frequently occurring adjectives.

continued

continued from previous

Speaking and Listening Standards	Language Standards
	g. Use frequently occurring conjunctions (e.g., *and, but, or, so, because*).
	h. Use determiners (e.g., articles, demonstratives).
	i. Use frequently occurring prepositions (e.g., *during, beyond, toward*).
	j. Produce and expand complete simple and compound declarative, interrogative, imperative, and exclamatory sentences in response to prompts
1 SL.1.6: Produce complete sentences when appropriate to task and situation. (See grade 1 Language standards 1 and 3 for specific expectations.)	**1 L.1.2:** Demonstrate command of the conventions of standard English capitalization, punctuation, and spelling when writing.
	a. Capitalize dates and names of people.
	b. Use end punctuation for sentences.
	c. Use commas in dates and to separate single words in a series.
	d. Use conventional spelling for words with common spelling patterns and for frequently occurring irregular words.
	e. Spell untaught words phonetically, drawing on phonemic awareness and spelling conventions.
	1 L.1.6: Use words and phrases acquired through conversations, reading and being read to, and responding to texts, including using frequently occurring conjunctions to signal simple relationships (e.g., *because*).
2 SL.2.4: Tell a story or recount an experience with appropriate facts and relevant, descriptive details, speaking audibly in coherent sentences.	**2 L.2.1:** Demonstrate command of the conventions of standard English grammar and usage when writing or speaking.
a. Plan and deliver a narrative presentation that: recounts a well-elaborated event, includes details, reflects a logical sequence, and provides a conclusion.	a. Use collective nouns (e.g., *group*).
	b. Form and use frequently occurring irregular plural nouns (e.g., *feet, children, teeth, mice, fish*).
	c. Use reflexive pronouns (e.g., *myself, ourselves*).
	d. Form and use the past tense of frequently occurring irregular verbs (e.g., *sat, hid, told*).
	e. Use adjectives and adverbs, and choose between them depending on what is to be modified.
	f. Produce, expand, and rearrange complete simple and compound sentences (e.g., *The boy watched the movie; The little boy watched the movie; The action movie was watched by the little boy*).
	g. Create readable documents with legible print.

continued from previous

Speaking and Listening Standards	Language Standards
2 **SL.2.6:** Produce complete sentences when appropriate to task and situation in order to provide requested detail or clarification. (See grade 2 Language standards 1 and 3 for specific expectations.)	**2** **L.2.2:** Demonstrate command of the conventions of standard English capitalization, punctuation, and spelling when writing. a. Capitalize holidays, product names, and geographic names. b. Use commas in greetings and closings of letters. c. Use an apostrophe to form contractions and frequently occurring possessives. d. Generalize learned spelling patterns when writing words (e.g., *cage—badge; boy—boil*). e. Consult reference materials, including beginning dictionaries, as needed to check and correct spellings.
	2 **L.2.3:** Use knowledge of language and its conventions when writing, speaking, reading, or listening. a. Compare formal and informal uses of English.
	2 **L.2.6:** Use words and phrases acquired through conversations, reading and being read to, and responding to texts, including using adjectives and adverbs to describe (e.g., *When other kids are happy that makes me happy*).

In addition to the ELA Language and Speaking/Listening standards provided in this chart, ELD Standard 11: Supporting opinions is **also** correlated with ELA Writing standards K.1, K.4, 1.1, 1.4, 2.1, 2.4, and 2.10.

Source: *Common Core State Standards, K–12 English Language Arts* (2010).

Notes

What the **Teacher** Does

Children write opinion pieces, informative or explanatory texts, and narratives. To meet grade-level expectations for opinion pieces such as responses to literature, children learn to state an opinion and provide a reason and some sense of closure (W.1.1) (p. 243).

Teachers can assist students with offering opinions and providing good reasons and referring to the text or to relevant background knowledge:

- Modeling how to state an opinion, and provide evidence for that opinion, by using a think aloud about a familiar text. The teacher can provide her opinion using a sentence frame, "*I believe that _____ because _____,*" and can demonstrate for students under a document camera where in the text she obtained support for her opinion. Students can then try the same exercise using the sentence frame and their own evidence from the text.

- Having students discuss opinions about personal or familiar topics, and providing evidence for those statements using sentence frames.

- Placing opinions about familiar topics on the board or sentence strips, and having students evaluate if the reasons and/or textual evidence adequately supports the statement.

- Having students rank each other's evidence to support an opinion on a scale of 1 to 5 (1 being lowest and 5 being highest). Sentences with the lowest rankings can be rewritten with a partner.

Tips for Differentiation by Proficiency Level

- **Emerging**—At the emerging level, students can provide opinions about familiar topics, such as their favorite food, using the sentence frame, "*I believe that ___ because _____*" to ensure that students provide evidence for their opinion. The teacher can chart student responses using Post-its and students' names.

- **Expanding**—At the expanding level, students can begin providing opinions about a familiar text, which perhaps has been read several times.

- **Bridging**—At the bridging level, students can provide opinions about a familiar text. The student can find several reasons to support their opinion.

Source: 2014 ELA/ELD Framework, p. 243.

Notes

Academic Vocabulary—Key Words and Phrases Related to Standard 11: Supporting opinions

Background knowledge: Using information already known, by prior study or personal experience, in order to better understand an idea or topic.

Evidence: Providing the facts or details to support an argument or opinion, including quotations, examples, photographs, expert opinions, and personal experience. Strong evidence provides credibility to the opinion or argument one is making.

Offering opinions: Using facts, reasons and evidence to come to a belief, conclusion, or judgment about a topic or issue.

Response to literature: Stating an opinion about a character's traits, the setting, plot, theme, or moral of the story. Typically, the response to literature is organized with a brief summary of the story, followed by an opinion that is supported by evidence from the text.

Source: Taberski & Burke, (2014), *The Common Core Companion: The Standards Decoded, Grades K–2.*

Notes

Example of Practice in Snapshot Related to Standard 11: Supporting opinions

---

Snapshot 3.11. Expanding Sentences and Building Vocabulary Designated ELD Connected to ELA/Social Studies in Grade 1

Because Mr. Dupont's EL children are at the Bridging level of English language proficiency, during designated ELD, he provides his students with extended opportunities to discuss their ideas and opinions, as he knows that this will support them later when writing down their ideas. He strategically targets particular language that he would like students to use in their opinion pieces by constructing sentence frames that contain specific vocabulary and grammatical structures that will enable his students to be more precise and detailed (e.g., "*My favorite hero is _____ because _____.*" "*_____ was very courageous when _____.*"). He explains to the children how they can expand their ideas in different ways by adding information about where, when, how, and so forth. For example, he explains that instead of simply saying, "*She worked on a farm,*" children could say, "*She worked on a farm in California,*" or they could add even more detail and precision by saying, "*She worked on a farm in the central valley of California.*" He provides his students with many opportunities to construct these expanded sentence structures as the students discuss the historical figures they are learning about and then write short summaries of their discussions at the end of each lesson. During these lessons, he encourages the children to refer to the texts they have previously read together and to cite evidence from them to support their ideas.

CA ELD Standards (Bridging): ELD.PI.K–1.1, 3, 6, 10, 12b; ELD.PII.K–1.4–5, 6
CA CCSS for ELA/Literacy: RI.1.1; SL.1.1, 4, 6; L.1.6

The snapshots and vignettes cited above can be found in their entirety at https://www.cde.ca.gov/ci/rl/cf/, *ELA/ELD Framework*, p. 260.

Notes

Emerging

K a. Retell texts and recount experiences using a select set of key words.

b. Use a select number of general academic and domain-specific words to add detail (e.g., adding the word *spicy* to describe a favorite food, using the word *larva* when explaining insect metamorphosis) while speaking and composing.

1 a. Retell texts and recount experiences, using key words.

b. Use a select number of general academic and domain-specific words to add detail (e.g., adding the word *scrumptious* to describe a favorite food, using the word *thorax* to refer to insect anatomy) while speaking and writing.

2 a. Retell texts and recount experiences by using key words.

b. Use a select number of general academic and domain-specific words to add detail (e.g., adding the word *generous* to describe a character, using the word *lava* to explain volcanic eruptions) while speaking and writing.

Expanding

K a. Retell texts and recount experiences using *complete sentences* and key words.

b. Use a *growing number of general academic and domain-specific words* in order to add detail *or to create shades of meaning (e.g., using the word scurry versus run)* while speaking and composing.

1 a. Retell texts and recount experiences, *using complete sentences* and key words.

b. Use a *growing number of* general academic and domain-specific words in order to add detail, *create an effect (e.g., using the word suddenly to signal a change), or create shades of meaning (e.g., prance versus walk)* while speaking and writing.

2 a. Retell texts and recount experiences *using complete sentences* and key words.

b. Use a *growing number of* general academic and domain-specific words in order to add detail, *create an effect (e.g., using the word suddenly to signal a change), or create shades of meaning (e.g., scurry versus dash)* while speaking and writing.

Bridging

K a. Retell texts and recount experiences using *increasingly detailed complete sentences* and key words.

b. Use a *wide variety* of general academic and domain-specific words, *synonyms, antonyms, and non-literal language to create an effect (e.g., using the word suddenly to signal a change)* or to create shades of meaning (e.g., *The cat's fur was as white as snow*) while speaking and composing.

1 a. Retell texts and recount experiences, using *increasingly detailed complete sentences* and key words.

b. Use *a wide variety of* general academic and domain-specific words, *synonyms, antonyms, and non-literal language (e.g., The dog was as big as a house) to create an effect, precision, and shades of meaning* while speaking and writing.

2 a. Retell texts and recount experiences using *increasingly detailed* complete sentences and key words.

b. *Use a wide variety* of general academic and domain-specific words, *synonyms, antonyms, and non-literal language (e.g., He was as quick as a cricket) to create an effect, precision,* and shades of meaning while speaking and writing.

Script *in bold italics* indicates content not found in earlier proficiency levels of the same ELD Standard.

Source: *California English Language Development Standards for Grades K–12,* California Department of Education (2012).

What the **Student** Does

Emerging	Expanding	Bridging

Gist: *Students can retell texts and recount experiences using complete sentences and key words. Students can use a number of general academic and domain-specific words in order to add detail while speaking and composing.*

K They consider:

- What do I want to include in my retell about this topic?
- Am I using complete sentences?
- Can I add detail to my retell by using key words?

K They *also* consider:

- Where can I add a detail using words from this subject area?

K They *also* consider:

- When I reread my writing now, does it make more sense to me?

Gist: *Students can retell texts and recount experiences using complete sentences and key words. Students can use a variety of general academic and domain-specific words in order to add detail and create shades of meaning while speaking and writing.*

1 They consider:

- What do I want to include in my retell about this topic?
- Am I using complete sentences?
- Can I add detail to my retell by using key words?

1 They *also* consider:

- What are some related details that help make sense for my audience?
- Do I have examples from the text that also add meaning?

1 They *also* consider:

- When I reread my writing now, have I created more meaning through the details and examples I have chosen?

Gist: *Students can retell texts and recount experiences using complete detailed sentences and key words. Students can use a wide variety of general academic and domain-specific words in order to add detail, precision, and create shades of meaning while speaking and writing.*

2 They consider:

- What are some related details that help make sense for my audience?
- Do I have examples from the text that also add meaning?

2 They *also* consider:

- Have I created more meaning through the details and examples I have chosen?

2 They *also* consider:

- When I reread my writing now, have I created more precision in my retell through the details and examples I have chosen?

Speaking and Listening Standards	Language Standards
K SL.K.4: Describe familiar people, places, things, and events and, with prompting and support, provide additional detail.	**K L.K.1:** Demonstrate command of the conventions of standard English grammar and usage when writing or speaking. a. Print many upper- and lowercase letters. b. Use frequently occurring nouns and verbs. c. Form regular plural nouns orally by adding /s/ or /es/ (e.g., *dog, dogs; wish, wishes*). d. Understand and use question words (interrogatives) (e.g., *who, what, where, when, why, how*). e. Use the most frequently occurring prepositions (e.g., *to, from, in, out, on, off, for, of, by, with*). f. Produce and expand complete sentences in shared language activities.
K SL.K.6: Speak audibly and express thoughts, feelings, and ideas clearly.	**K L.K.5:** With guidance and support from adults, explore word relationships and nuances in word meanings. a. Sort common objects into categories (e.g., shapes, foods) to gain a sense of the concepts the categories represent. b. Demonstrate understanding of frequently occurring verbs and adjectives by relating them to their opposites (antonyms). c. Identify real-life connections between words and their use (e.g., note places at school that are colorful). d. Distinguish shades of meaning among verbs describing the same general action (e.g., *walk, march, strut, prance*) by acting out the meanings.
	K L.K.6: Use words and phrases acquired through conversations, reading and being read to, and responding to texts.
1 SL.1.4: Describe people, places, things, and events with relevant details, expressing ideas and feelings clearly. a. Memorize and recite poems, rhymes, and songs with expression.	**1 L.1.1:** Demonstrate command of the conventions of standard English grammar and usage when writing or speaking. a. Print all upper- and lowercase letters. b. Use common, proper, and possessive nouns. c. Use singular and plural nouns with matching verbs in basic sentences (e.g., *He hops; We hop*). d. Use personal (subject, object), possessive, and indefinite pronouns (e.g., *I, me, my; they, them, their; anyone, everything*).

continued

continued from previous

Speaking and Listening Standards	Language Standards
	e. Use verbs to convey a sense of past, present, and future (e.g., *Yesterday I walked home; Today I walk home; Tomorrow I will walk home*). f. Use frequently occurring adjectives. g. Use frequently occurring conjunctions (e.g., *and, but, or, so, because*). h. Use determiners (e.g., articles, demonstratives). i. Use frequently occurring prepositions (e.g., *during, beyond, toward*). j. Produce and expand complete simple and compound declarative, interrogative, imperative, and exclamatory sentences in response to prompts.
1 **SL.1.6:** Produce complete sentences when appropriate to task and situation. (See grade 1 Language standards 1 and 3 for specific expectations.)	**1** **L.1.5:** With guidance and support from adults, demonstrate understanding of word relationships and nuances in word meanings. a. Sort words into categories (e.g., colors, clothing) to gain a sense of the concepts the categories represent. b. Define words by category and by one or more key attributes (e.g., *a duck is a bird that swims; a tiger is a large cat with stripes*). c. Identify real-life connections between words and their use (e.g., note places at home that are cozy). d. Distinguish shades of meaning among verbs differing in manner (e.g., *look, peek, glance, stare, glare, scowl*) and adjectives differing in intensity (e.g., *large, gigantic*) by defining or choosing them or by acting out the meanings.
	1 **L.1.6:** Use words and phrases acquired through conversations, reading and being read to, and responding to texts, including using frequently occurring conjunctions to signal simple relationships (e.g., *because*).
2 **SL.2.4:** Tell a story or recount an experience with appropriate facts and relevant, descriptive details, speaking audibly in coherent sentences. a. Plan and deliver a narrative presentation that: recounts a well-elaborated event, includes details, reflects a logical sequence, and provides a conclusion.	**2** **L.2.1:** Demonstrate command of the conventions of standard English grammar and usage when writing or speaking. a. Use collective nouns (e.g., *group*). b. Form and use frequently occurring irregular plural nouns (e.g., *feet, children, teeth, mice, fish*). c. Use reflexive pronouns (e.g., *myself, ourselves*). d. Form and use the past tense of frequently occurring irregular verbs (e.g., *sat, hid, told*). e. Use adjectives and adverbs, and choose between them depending on what is to be modified.

continued from previous

Speaking and Listening Standards	Language Standards
	f. Produce, expand, and rearrange complete simple and compound sentences (e.g., The boy watched the movie; The little boy watched the movie; The action movie was watched by the little boy). g. Create readable documents with legible print.
2 **SL.2.6:** Produce complete sentences when appropriate to task and situation in order to provide requested detail or clarification. (See grade 2 Language standards 1 and 3 for specific expectations.)	**2** **L.2.3:** Use knowledge of language and its conventions when writing, speaking, reading, or listening. a. Compare formal and informal uses of English.
	2 **L.2.5:** Demonstrate understanding of word relationships and nuances in word meanings. a. I dentify real-life connections between words and their use (e.g., describe foods that are spicy or juicy). b. Distinguish shades of meaning among closely related verbs (e.g., *toss, throw, hurl*) and closely related adjectives (e.g., *thin, slender, skinny, scrawny*).
	2 **L.2.6:** Use words and phrases acquired through conversations, reading and being read to, and responding to texts, including using adjectives and adverbs to describe (e.g., *When other kids are happy that makes me happy*).

In addition to the ELA Language and Speaking/Listening standards provided in this chart, ELD Standard 12: *Selecting language resources* is **also** correlated with ELA Writing standards K.5, 1.5, 2.4, and 2.5.

Source: *Common Core State Standards, K–12 English Language Arts* (2010).

Notes

What the **Teacher** Does

As noted in previous sections, language undergirds literacy and learning, and children's command of academic language in particular is related to present and future achievement. Serious attention is given to developing children's language, yet instruction is age appropriate and meaning based. In other words, new vocabulary and complex sentence structures are relevant for [this age group] and serve real purposes: to understand and appreciate increasingly complex texts, learn new concepts and information in the content areas, and communicate effectively and precisely (p. 241).

Teachers can assist students with retelling texts and recounting experiences using complete sentences and key words. Students can use a number of general academic and domain-specific words in order to add detail while speaking and composing:

- Building background knowledge around new words by providing experiences with short texts or videos, a series of pictures, or hands-on experiences that connects to those words.

- Using a strategy like the Frayer model (see Example of Practice Snapshot 3.9), where students write down examples, non-examples (or synonyms and antonyms), draw a visual, in order to develop their own definition of a word. This strategy teaches many words as associated with one key concept or target word, so that students are learning many words at one time.

- Selecting key Tier 2 words, which are high-utility words that go across content areas, or Tier 3 words, which are domain- or discipline-specific words, to teach directly and connect to students' reading, writing, key standards, or essential questions.

- Having students create idiom dictionaries with literal and figurative meanings, as well as pictures of those meanings.

- Having students sort words that have shades of meaning (*scurry* vs. *dash*) from least to most impactful, and asking them to justify why they organized their words in the order that they decided.

- Assisting students with metalinguistic awareness, including the understanding that words and sentences can have more than one meaning, which can improve comprehension and allow them to think about the appropriate meaning. Teachers can use Peggy Parish's *Amelia Bedelia* series for this.

Tips for Differentiation by Proficiency Level

- *Emerging*—At the emerging level, students can retell familiar or personal experiences or texts using sentence frames that assist with beginning their responses such as, *"The story was about _____ and ____."*

- *Expanding*—At the expanding level, students can work in pairs or small groups to retell parts of a familiar story together. One student can retell the beginning, another student can retell the middle, and a third student can retell the end of the story.

- *Bridging*—At the bridging level, students can retell a familiar text using a more sophisticated sentence frame, such as *"The story was about _____ and ____. First, ____ and then, _____. Lastly, _____."*

Source: 2014 ELA/ELD Framework, p. 241.

Academic Vocabulary—Key Words and Phrases Related to Standard 12: Selecting
language resources

Antonyms: Using words which are opposite in meaning to other words and may add shades of meaning to a student's speech or writing. For example, *poor* is an antonym of *rich*, but may evoke more imagery than just saying, *"He was not rich."*

Create precision: Using words which specifically describe the idea or topic (e.g., *scurry* instead of *run*).

Details to strengthen writing: Adding details, examples, and elaboration that add specifics to the ideas and/or topic.

Domain-specific vocabulary: Using the words which relate specifically to a subject area, such as *associative* for math and *hypothesis* for science. The correct use of domain-specific words in presentations and writing add credibility and precision to what the student is saying.

Frayer model: Using a graphic organizer for word analysis and vocabulary building. This four-square model prompts students to think about and describe the meaning of a word or concept in terms of definition, characteristics, examples and non-examples.

Non-literal language: Using language that goes beyond the dictionary meaning of the word or phrase. Writers use non-literal language to help readers picture or understand something. A common example of non-literal language is the use of idioms, such as, *as scared as a jackrabbit.*

Shades of meaning: Using words which may be synonyms of other, more familiar words, but which bring a sense of specificity to the sentence (e.g., *fragile* instead of *weak*).

Synonyms: Using words which are similar in meaning to other words, and may add precision to a student's speech or writing. For example, *gallop* is a synonym of *run*, but is more vivid and precise about the kind of movement being made.

Source: Taberski & Burke, (2014), *The Common Core Companion: The Standards Decoded, Grades K–2.*

Notes

Example of Practice in Snapshot Related to Standard 12: Selecting language resources

Snapshot 3.9. Teaching Science Vocabulary Integrated ELA, ELD, and Science in Grade 1

After initial teaching that included child-friendly definitions at point of contact (while reading texts aloud to students or discussing science concepts), Mr. Rodriguez selects several domain-specific words from the students' ongoing study of life cycles for deeper exploration. One word he selects is *metamorphosis* because it represents a crucial concept in the content. He asks students to think about where they had heard the word during their study, and with his assistance, they recall that it was used in the book about caterpillars changing into moths and in the time-lapse video clip showing tadpoles becoming frogs. On large chart paper, he draws a graphic known as a Frayer Model. He writes the target word in the center and labels the four quadrants. He reminds the students of the definition—it was one they had discussed many times—and asks them to share with a neighbor something they know about the concept after the recent few weeks of investigation. Next, he records the definition generated with the children's assistance in one quadrant of the chart.

Mr. Rodriguez then asks students to reflect on their learning and offer some examples of animals that undergo metamorphosis, recording their contributions in the appropriate places on the chart. Importantly, he also asks for examples of animals that do not undergo metamorphosis, thus better supporting concept development. Finally, he supports the children in identifying some characteristics of metamorphosis. What does it entail? What are some important aspects of metamorphosis? As he asks each of these questions, he provides students with sufficient time to turn and talk in triads about their ideas. He supports his EL students' participation and engagement in the conversations with sentence frames (e.g., *"One thing that's important about metamorphosis is _____."*).

CA CCSS for ELA/Literacy: L.1.1–2, 5; SL.1.1, 2, 4

CA ELD Standards: ELD.PI.1.1–3, 6, 9, 12b; ELD.PII.1.6

The snapshots and vignettes cited above can be found in their entirety at https://www.cde.ca.gov/ci/rl/cf/, *ELA/ELD Framework*, p. 255.

Notes

Part 2

LEARNING ABOUT HOW ENGLISH WORKS

A *Structuring Cohesive Texts*

Introduction

Part II of the *California ELD Standards* promotes English Language Learners' abilities to *learn about how English works* so that they acquire knowledge about English and their abilities to use English in order to be successful in school. Part II **comes second in the standards** so that ELLs can use their awareness of how English works to make meaning, comprehend, and produce language in various ways and in a range of content areas. Part II, Learning About How English Works, is organized into the following ways of using language meaningfully:

A. Structuring Cohesive Texts

- *Understanding text structure and organization* based on purpose, text type, and discipline
- *Understanding cohesion and how language resources* across a text contribute to the way a text unfolds and flows

B. Expanding and Enriching Ideas

- *Using verbs and verb phrases* to create precision and clarity in different text types
- *Using nouns and noun phrases* to expand ideas and provide more detail
- *Modifying to add details* to provide more information and create precision

C. Connecting and Condensing Ideas

- *Connecting ideas* within sentences by combining clauses
- *Condensing ideas* within sentences using a variety of language resources

Cluster A: Structuring Cohesive Texts Standards have the same general descriptions K–12 for the two standards in the cluster. These include

1. *Understanding text structure and organization based on purpose, text type, and discipline.* Students, especially ELLs, need to be explicitly taught the purpose, organizational structure, and linguistic features of a variety of text types, including narrative, informational, and argumentation, during both reading and writing. ELLs will need to read and be provided with model texts, as well as the connectives or transition words, that are associated with the text type expected of them. Teachers may choose to jointly construct pieces with their students to provide modeling or support before independent practice with writing (Gibbons, 2002; Soto, 2014).

2. *Understanding cohesion and how language resources across a text contribute to the way a text unfolds and flows.* Students also need to understand how writers and speakers make their texts cohesive.

Cohesion refers to how information unfolds, or flows, throughout a text and how the text "hangs together." A cohesive text is created through the selection of a variety of language resources, such as referring back or forward in the text to people, ideas, or things using pronouns or synonyms, in order to signal shifts in meaning in the text, among other cohesive language resources (ELA/ELD Framework Appendix B, 2012, p. 10).

In this document, the section on What the Student Does provides specific descriptions of competence with each of the Structuring Cohesive Text standards at the appropriate grade range and proficiency level. Similarly, the section on What the Teacher Does provides specific strategies for developing competence with each of the Structuring Cohesive Text standards at the appropriate grade range.

Source: *California English Language Development Standards, K–12* (2012). Appendix B, "The California English Language Development Standards Part I: Learning About How English Works," provides an excellent summary of the research used in developing Part II of the standards.

Emerging	Expanding	Bridging
K Apply understanding of how text types are organized (e.g., how a story is organized by a sequence of events) to comprehending and composing texts in shared language activities guided by the teacher, with peers, and sometimes independently.	**K** Apply understanding of how ***different*** text types are organized ***to express ideas*** (e.g., how a story is organized ***sequentially with predictable stages versus how an informative text is organized by topic and details***) to comprehending and composing texts in shared language activities guided by the teacher, ***collaboratively*** with peers, and with ***increasing independence***.	**K** Apply understanding of how different text types are organized ***predictably*** (e.g., a narrative text versus an informative text ***versus an opinion text***) to comprehending and composing texts in shared language activities guided by the teacher, with peers, and ***independently***.
1 Apply understanding of how text types are organized (e.g., how a story is organized by a sequence of events) to comprehending and composing basic texts with substantial support (e.g., using drawings, through joint construction with a peer or teacher) to comprehending texts and writing texts in shared language activities guided by the teacher, with peers, and sometimes independently.	**1** Apply understanding of how ***different*** text types are organized ***to express ideas*** (e.g., how a story is organized ***sequentially with predictable stages versus how an informative text is organized by topic and details***) to comprehending texts and writing texts in shared language activities guided by the teacher, with peers, and with ***increasing independence***.	**1** Apply understanding of how different text types are organized ***predictably*** (e.g., how a story is organized **versus an *informative/explanatory* text versus an *opinion text***) to comprehending texts and writing texts in shared language activities guided by the teacher and ***independently***.
2 Apply understanding of how different text types are organized to express ideas (e.g., how a story is organized sequentially) to comprehending and composing texts in shared language activities guided by the teacher, with peers, and sometimes independently.	**2** Apply understanding of how different text types are organized to express ideas (e.g., how a story is organized sequentially ***with predictable stages versus how an informative text is organized by topic and details***) to comprehending texts and composing texts with ***increasing independence***.	**2** Apply understanding of how different text types are organized ***predictably*** to express ideas (e.g., ***a narrative versus an informative/explanatory text versus an opinion text***) to comprehending texts and writing texts ***independently***.

Script ***in bold italics*** indicates content not found in earlier proficiency levels of the same ELD Standard.

Source: *California English Language Development Standards for Grades K–12*, California Department of Education (2012).

What the **Student** Does

Emerging	Expanding	Bridging

Gist: *Students understand how different text types are organized to express ideas and can comprehend and compose texts in shared language activities guided by the teacher, with peers, and with some independence.*

K They consider:

- What kind of a text am I looking at?
- Can I work with the teacher and/or other students to compose a text of a certain type?

K They *also* consider:

- Do I know how stories and information texts are organized differently?

K They *also* consider:

- Do I know how narratives, information texts, and opinion texts are organized differently?
- Can I work on my own to compose a text of a certain type?

Gist: *Students understand how different text types are organized to express ideas and can comprehend and compose texts in shared language activities guided by the teacher, and with increasing independence.*

1 They consider:

- What kind of a text is this?
- Can we use drawings or other illustrations to help express our ideas?
- Can I work with the teacher and/or other students to compose a text of a certain type?

1 They *also* consider:

- Do I know how stories and information texts are organized differently?

1 They *also* consider:

- Do I know how narratives, information texts, and opinion texts are organized differently?
- Can I work on my own to compose a text of a certain type?

Gist: *Students understand how different text types are organized to express ideas and can comprehend and compose texts independently.*

2 They consider:

- What kind of a text is this?
- Can I work with the teacher and/or other students to compose a text of a certain type?
- How much can I do on my own to compose a text?

2 They *also* consider:

- Do I know how stories and information texts are organized differently?
- How independently can I work to compose a text?

2 They *also* consider:

- Do I know how narratives, information texts, and opinion texts are organized differently?
- Can I work on my own to compose a text of a certain type?

Source: California English Language Development Standards for Grades K–12 (2012).

Speaking and Listening Standards	Language Standards
K **SL.K.4:** Describe familiar people, places, things, and events and, with prompting and support, provide additional detail.	
1 **SL.1.4:** Describe people, places, things, and events with relevant details, expressing ideas and feelings clearly. a. Memorize and recite poems, rhymes, and songs with expression.	
2 **SL.2.4:** Tell a story or recount an experience with appropriate facts and relevant, descriptive details, speaking audibly in coherent sentences. a. Plan and deliver a narrative presentation that: recounts a well-elaborated event, includes details, reflects a logical sequence, and provides a conclusion.	

In addition to the ELA Speaking/Listening standards provided on this chart, ELD Standard 1: Understanding text structure is **also** correlated with ELA Reading Literature and Information standards K.5, 1.5, and 2.5, and Writing standards K.1–3, K.5, 1.1–3, 1.5, and 2.1–5.

Source: *Common Core State Standards, K–12 English Language Arts* (2010).

Notes

What the **Teacher** Does

Teachers are well versed in high-quality children's literature of all genres; each genre, including fiction, can contribute to children's knowledge. They have ample selections, in English and in the languages of the children, available to share with children, both as read alouds and for independent exploration.

The CA CCSS for ELA/Literacy include ten standards in the Reading strand that focus on reading informational text (RI.K–1, Standards 1–10). These standards underscore the importance of building children's skill with this genre. Informational text is a valuable source of knowledge. However, engaging with informational texts, though crucial, does not replace the learning experiences and investigations that are essential aspects of content instruction. Instead, it complements them (p. 149).

Teachers can assist students with understanding how different text types are organized to express ideas and comprehend and compose texts in shared language activities guided by the teacher, with peers, and with some independence:

- Selecting high-interest, culturally responsive texts of various genres to read with their ELLs, in order to unpack text structure and text features.
- Explicitly introducing the organizational structure, linguistic features, and linking words associated with each text type, so that students become familiar with them as they are reading.
- Charting examples of the organizational structure, linguistic features, and linking words associated with a familiar text read to students more than one time.
- Having students circle and underline the organizational structure, linguistic features, and linking words associated with a familiar text as the teacher reads the text aloud to students.
- Jointly construct a text with the teacher or a partner using the organizational structure, linguistic features, and linking words previously taught, as well as sentence frames to begin each segment of the text.
- Working with students to address language (vocabulary, grammar and syntax, and text structure and genre) at the text and/or discourse level.

Tips for Differentiation by Proficiency Level

- **Emerging**—Teachers can select and read aloud shorter, high-interest texts with repetition in order to teach text structure with students. Teachers should begin with narrative text, as this is often more accessible. Teachers can ask students to repeat the common phrases in the text so that they interact with the text structure as it is read aloud to them. Teachers should also read the texts several times to students.
- **Expanding**—At the expanding level, teachers can select narrative texts with a bit more complexity and continue to highlight text structure throughout a read aloud. Teachers can chart the elements of the text structure as they appear in the text.
- **Bridging**—At the bridging level, teachers can read aloud informational texts, and highlight and chart the text features associated with the text type. After the teacher has read the text aloud to students, in pairs, students can reread the text together, via a shared reading.

Source: 2014 ELA/ELD Framework, p. 149.

Academic Vocabulary—Key Words and Phrases Related to Standard 1: Understanding text structure

Analyze the structure of texts: Looking at how authors organize their ideas, depending on the text type. Structural patterns at the sentence, paragraph, and whole-text level follow predicable patterns according to the text type.

Culturally responsive texts: Demonstrating the importance of including students' cultural references in their learning materials, such as positive perspectives on parents and families, communication of high expectations, and learning within the context of culture.

Informative/explanatory texts: Writing types that give information or explanations about topics, using facts and an objective tone.

Joint construction: Working together to design a piece of writing, taking responsibility for individual parts, offering responses to each other's writing, and combining all the parts into one cohesive text.

Predictable organization of texts: Referring to the organization of types of texts. For example, narrative texts occur in a time sequence of things that happen, while informational texts follow a predictable organization of main ideas, supporting ideas, and conclusion.

Shared language activities: Developing understanding within a team or classroom based on language (e.g., spoken, text, body language, or visuals) in a way that helps them communicate more effectively. This may be simply explaining to another the meaning of a locally used term, or more extensively it may be a level of engagement and interaction that takes months, possibly years to develop.

Text types: Under the general headings of literary and information texts, there are subcategories such as stories, drama, and poetry, literary nonfiction, and historical, scientific, and technical texts.

Source: Taberski & Burke, (2014), *The Common Core Companion: The Standards Decoded, Grades K–2.*

Notes

Example of Practice in Snapshot Related to Standard 1: Understanding text structure

Snapshot 3.2. *Goldilocks and the Three Bears* **Integrated ELA and ELD in Transitional Kindergarten**

Transitional kindergarteners listen to, enjoy, and discuss the book *Goldilocks and the Three Bears* several times over the course of a week. They chant along when there are repetitive phrases, ask and answer questions about the story, and talk about the illustrations. Their teacher, Mrs. Haddad, guides children's identification of key story details by using its narrative structure and recording the characters, settings, and events of the plot on a large chart. With support, children use 12″ × 18″ construction paper to construct individual books. Drawing or using cut paper, each child designs a cover page, a page with a home in the forest, a third page with three bowls, a fourth with three chairs, and a fifth page with three beds. Paper cutouts of Goldilocks and the bears are given to the children to use as props. The children move the props through the pages of their books as they read, using the cutouts as scaffolds as they retell the story to one another.

CA CCSS for ELA/Literacy: RL.K.1–3; W.K.3; SL.K.1–2; L.K.6
CA ELD Standards: ELD.PI.K.12a; ELD.PII.K.1, 2, 3b

The snapshots and vignettes cited above can be found in their entirety at https://www.cde.ca.gov/ci/rl/cf/, *ELA/ELD Framework*, p. 186.

Notes

Emerging

K Apply basic understanding of how ideas, events, or reasons are linked throughout a text using more everyday connecting words or phrases (e.g., *one time, then*) to comprehending texts and composing texts in shared language activities guided by the teacher, with peers, and sometimes independently.

1 Apply basic understanding of how ideas, events, or reasons are linked throughout a text using more everyday connecting words or phrases (e.g., *one day, after, then*) to comprehending texts and writing texts in shared language activities guided by the teacher, with peers, and sometimes independently.

2 Apply basic understanding of how ideas, events, or reasons are linked throughout a text using more everyday connecting words or phrases (e.g., *today, then*) to comprehending texts and composing texts in shared language activities guided by the teacher, with peers, and sometimes independently.

Expanding

K Apply understanding of how ideas, events, or reasons are linked throughout a text using a ***growing number of*** connecting words or phrases (e.g., ***next, after a long time***) to comprehending texts and composing texts in shared language activities guided by the teacher, with peers, and with ***increasing independence***.

1 Apply understanding of how ideas, events, or reasons are linked throughout a text using a ***growing number of*** connecting words or phrases (e.g., a ***long time ago, suddenly***) to comprehending texts and writing texts in shared language activities guided by the teacher and with ***increasing independence***.

2 Apply understanding of how ideas, events, or reasons are linked throughout a text using a ***growing number of*** connecting words or phrases (e.g., ***after a long time, first/ next***) to comprehending texts with ***increasing independence***.

Bridging

K Apply understanding of how ideas, events, or reasons are linked throughout a text using a ***variety*** of connecting words or phrases (e.g., ***first/ second/third, once, at the end***) to comprehending texts and composing texts in shared language activities guided by the teacher, with peers, and ***independently***.

1 Apply understanding of how ideas, events, or reasons are linked throughout a text using a ***variety of*** connecting words or phrases (e.g., ***for example, after that, first/second/third***) to comprehending texts and composing texts in shared language activities guided by the teacher, with peers and ***independently***.

2 Apply understanding of how ideas, events, or reasons are linked throughout a text using a ***variety of*** connecting words or phrases (e.g., ***for example, after that, suddenly***) to comprehending texts and writing texts ***independently***.

Script ***in bold italics*** indicates content not found in earlier proficiency levels of the same ELD Standard.

Source: *California English Language Development Standards for Grades K–12*, California Department of Education (2012).

What the **Student** Does

Emerging	Expanding	Bridging
Gist: *Students apply basic understanding of how ideas, events, or reasons are linked throughout a text using everyday connecting words or phrases to comprehending and composing texts in shared language activities guided by the teacher, with peers, and with some independence.*		
K They consider:	**K** They *also* consider:	**K** They *also* consider:
• What connecting words or phrases are in this text to help me? • Do these words link ideas, events, or reasons in the text? • Can I work with the teacher and/or other students to understand a text using connecting words?	• Can I work with the teacher and/or other students to compose a text using connecting words?	• Can I work on my own to compose a text using connecting words?
Gist: *Students apply understanding of how ideas, events, or reasons are linked throughout a text using a variety of connecting words or phrases to comprehending and writing texts in shared language activities guided by the teacher and with increasing independence.*		
1 They consider:	**1** They *also* consider:	**1** They *also* consider:
• What connecting words or phrases are in this text to help me? • Do these words link ideas, events, or reasons in the text? • Can I work with the teacher to understand a text using connecting words?	• Can I work with the teacher to compose a text using connecting words?	• Can I work on my own to compose a text using connecting words?
Gist: *Students apply understanding of how ideas, events, or reasons are linked throughout a text using a variety of connecting words or phrases to comprehending and writing texts independently.*		
2 They consider:	**2** They *also* consider:	**2** Same as Expanding.
• What connecting words or phrases are in this text to help me? • Do these words link ideas, events, or reasons in the text? • Can I work with the teacher to understand a text using connecting words?	• Can I work on my own to compose a text using connecting words?	

Source: *California English Language Development Standards for Grades K–12* (2012).

Speaking and Listening Standards	Language Standards
K **SL.K.4:** Describe familiar people, places, things, and events and, with prompting and support, provide additional detail.	**K** **L.K.1:** Demonstrate command of the conventions of standard English grammar and usage when writing or speaking. a. Print many upper- and lowercase letters. b. Use frequently occurring nouns and verbs. c. Form regular plural nouns orally by adding /s/ or /es/ (e.g., *dog, dogs; wish, wishes*). d. Understand and use question words (interrogatives) (e.g., *who, what, where, when, why, how*). e. Use the most frequently occurring prepositions (e.g., *to, from, in, out, on, off, for, of, by, with*). f. Produce and expand complete sentences in shared language activities.
1 **SL.1.4:** Describe people, places, things, and events with relevant details, expressing ideas and feelings clearly. a. Memorize and recide poems, rhymes, and songs with expression.	**1** **L.1.1:** Demonstrate command of the conventions of standard English grammar and usage when writing or speaking. a. Print all upper- and lowercase letters. b. Use common, proper, and possessive nouns. c. Use singular and plural nouns with matching verbs in basic sentences (e.g., *He hops; We hop*). d. Use personal (subject, object), possessive, and indefinite pronouns (e.g., *I, me, my; they, them, their; anyone, everything*). e. Use verbs to convey a sense of past, present, and future (e.g., *Yesterday I walked home; Today I walk home; Tomorrow I will walk home*). f. Use frequently occurring adjectives. g. Use frequently occurring conjunctions (e.g., *and, but, or, so, because*). h. Use determiners (e.g., articles, demonstratives). i. Use frequently occurring prepositions (e.g., *during, beyond, toward*). j. Produce and expand complete simple and compound declarative, interrogative, imperative, and exclamatory sentences in response to prompts.

continued

continued from previous

Speaking and Listening Standards	Language Standards
2 **SL.2.4:** Tell a story or recount an experience with appropriate facts and relevant, descriptive details, speaking audibly in coherent sentences. a. Plan and deliver a narrative presentation that: recounts a well-elaborated event, includes details, reflects a logical sequence, and provides a conclusion.	**2** **L.2.1:** Demonstrate command of the conventions of standard English grammar and usage when writing or speaking. a. Use collective nouns (e.g., *group*). b. Form and use frequently occurring irregular plural nouns (e.g., *feet, children, teeth, mice, fish*). c. Use reflexive pronouns (e.g., *myself, ourselves*). d. Form and use the past tense of frequently occurring irregular verbs (e.g., *sat, hid, told*). e. Use adjectives and adverbs, and choose between them depending on what is to be modified. f. Produce, expand, and rearrange complete simple and compound sentences (e.g., *The boy watched the movie; The little boy watched the movie; The action movie was watched by the little boy*). g. Create readable documents with legible print.
	2 **L.2.3:** Use knowledge of language and its conventions when writing, speaking, reading, or listening. a. Compare formal and informal uses of English.

In addition to the ELA Language and Speaking/Listening standards provided on this chart, ELD Standard 2: Understanding cohesion is also correlated with ELA Reading Literature and Reading Information standards K.5, 1.5, and 2.5, and Writing standards K.1–3, 5, 1.1–3, 5, and 2.1–4.

Source: *Common Core State Standards, K–12 English Language Arts* (2010).

Notes

What the **Teacher** Does

The CA ELD Standards serve as a guide to support ELLs' achievement toward effective expression in writing. They highlight and amplify skills that contribute to writing: Children learn through integrated and designated ELD about how texts are structured, how to expand their ideas using rich language, and how to connect their ideas within sentences and throughout entire texts to create more interesting, informative, or persuasive pieces of writing (p. 145).

Teachers can assist students with applying basic understanding of how ideas, events, or reasons are linked throughout a text using more everyday connecting words or phrases (e.g., *one time*, *then*) to comprehending texts and composing texts in shared language activities guided by the teacher, with peers, and sometimes independently:

- Introducing linking and transition words that are connected to each text type that has been read to students. For example, for importance, transitional words such as *first, second, third, mainly, more important, most of all, last but not least* can be taught. Teachers can create a chart for each text type that is introduced with its corresponding linking and transition words so that students can remember to use them in their own writing.

- Having students circle and underline and circle connecting words or phrases in a familiar text read aloud by the teacher.

- Using sentence strips to have students construct or reconstruct texts using connecting words or phrases in a familiar text. Students can then substitute other linking or transition words with new transition words.

- Using the linking or transition words that have been explicitly taught and underlined in a text, reconstruct or jointly construct a writing selection with the teacher.

- Using sentence frames with key linking or transition words previously taught, have students jointly construct a paragraph with a partner or the teacher.

Tips for Differentiation by Proficiency Level

- *Emerging* —At the emerging level, teachers can select model texts as read alouds and high-light the linking and transition words that are used by the author. The teacher can chart these words for the students so that they can use them in spoken language.

- *Expanding* —At the expanding level, teachers can underline linking and transition words used by an author using a document camera, and ask students to do the same with their texts (copies of the texts can be made for highlighting).

- *Bridging* —At the bridging level, after teachers and students have read texts together, they can place linking and transition words on Post-its, in order to create effective sentences, and then paragraphs, using those words.

Source: 2014 ELA/ELD Framework, p. 145.

Academic Vocabulary—Key Words and Phrases Related to Standard 2: Understanding cohesion

Cohesion: Forming a united whole from several parts. In the context of understanding and writing texts, this refers to using the predicable structure of a text type, using connecting words and phrases to link ideas, and using the domain-specific vocabulary to specify understanding.

Connecting words and phrases: Using phrases or words to connect one idea to the next in a text or presentation; connecting words (e.g., *first, last, after, then*) are used to help the reader progress from one significant idea to another. They build coherence in a text.

Reasons: Providing a cause, explanation, or justification for an action, event, or idea. Strong reasons are based in evidence from the text or prior knowledge.

Shared language activities: Developing understanding within a team or classroom based on language (e.g., spoken, text, body language, or visuals) in a way that helps them communicate more effectively. This may be simply explaining to another the meaning of a locally used term, or more extensively it may be a level of engagement and interaction that takes months, possibly years to develop.

Source: Taberski & Burke, (2014), *The Common Core Companion: The Standards Decoded, Grades K–2.*

Notes

Example of Practice in Snapshot Related to Standard 2: Understanding cohesion

Vignette 3.6. Unpacking Sentences Designated ELD Instruction in Grade 1

Mrs. Fabian helps her students unpack other sentences from the texts they are using in integrated ELA and science. Each one is a complex sentence containing the subordinate conjunctions *as* or *while*. She writes each sentence on chart paper, reads them with the students, and invites them to explain in their own words what is happening. Then she writes the students' simpler sentences down on the chart paper for all to see. During this process, she explicitly draws their attention to how the two ideas are connected using the words *as* and *while*, and she and the students engage in extensive discussion about the meaning of the original sentence.

CA ELD Standards (Expanding): ELD.PI.1—Contribute to class, group, and partner discussions by listening attentively, following turn-taking rules, and asking and answering questions; ELD.PI.7—Describe the language writers or speakers use to present or support an idea (e.g., the adjectives used to describe people and places) with prompting and moderate support; ELD.PII.6—Combine clauses in an increasing variety of ways to make connections between and to join ideas, for example, to express cause/effect (e.g., "She jumped because the dog barked."), in shared language activities guided by the teacher and with increasing independence.

The snapshots and vignettes cited above can be found in their entirety at https://www.cde.ca.gov/ci/rl/cf/, *ELA/ELD Framework*, p. 272.

Notes

Part 2

LEARNING ABOUT HOW ENGLISH WORKS

B *Expanding and Enriching Ideas*

Introduction

Part II of the *California ELD Standards* promotes English Language Learners' abilities to *learn about how English works* so that they acquire knowledge about English and their abilities to use English to be successful in school. Part II **comes second in the standards** so that ELLs can use their awareness of how English works to make meaning, comprehend, and produce language in various ways and in a range of content areas. Part II, Learning About How English Works, is organized into the following ways of using language meaningfully:

A. Structuring Cohesive Texts

- *Understanding text structure and organization* based on purpose, text type, and discipline
- *Understanding cohesion and how language resources* across a text contribute to the way a text unfolds and flows

B. Expanding and Enriching Ideas

- *Using verbs and verb phrases* to create precision and clarity in different text types
- *Using nouns and noun phrases* to expand ideas and provide more detail
- *Modifying to add details* to provide more information and create precision

C. Connecting and Condensing Ideas

- *Connecting ideas* within sentences by combining clauses
- *Condensing ideas* within sentences using a variety of language resources

---

Cluster B: Expanding and Enriching Ideas have the same general descriptions K–12 for the two standards in the cluster. *It is important to note that Part II, Cluster B of the standards especially should be taught in context to students' reading and writing, and not as isolated skills.* These include

1. *Using verbs and verb phrases* to create precision and clarity in different text types—ELLs can be taught how to become more precise and clear in their writing by using verbs and verb phrases. A verb phrase consists of an auxiliary, or helping, verb and main verb, including all its modifiers. The helping verb precedes the main verb. Helping verbs include forms of *be*, such as *am, is, are, was, were, being,* and *been*; forms of *have*, such as *has* and *had*; forms of *do*, such as *does* and *did*; forms of *can*, such as *could, will, would*, and *shall*; and forms of *should*, such as *may, might*, and *must*. Providing examples in context to students' reading and writing are the most helpful ways to teach this concept.

2. *Using nouns and noun phrases* to expand ideas and provide more detail—Teaching students how to expand nouns by adding modifiers is another way to assist students with becoming more detailed in their writing. Specifically, during ELD, teachers can model for students how to identify the "head noun," as well as the pre- and post-modifiers using sentence strips. Again, this should all be done in context to students' own reading or writing assignments (ELA/ELD Framework Appendix B, 2012, p. 15).

3. *Modifying to add details* to provide more information and create precision—Students can be taught how to expand sentences with adverbials (e.g., adverbs, adverb phrases, or prepositional phrases) to provide more detail, including time, manner, or place. This can be done by having students modify familiar texts, their own experiences, or their own writing.

The section on What the Student Does provides specific descriptions of competence with each of the Expanding and Enriching Ideas standards at the appropriate grade range and proficiency level. Similarly, the section on What the Teacher Does provides specific strategies for developing competence with each of the Expanding and Enriching Ideas standards at the appropriate grade range.

Source: *California English Language Development Standards, K–12* (2012). See Appendix B, "The California English Language Development Standards Part II: Learning About How English Works."

Emerging

K a. Use frequently used verbs (e.g., *go, eat, run*) and verb types (e.g., doing, saying, being/having, thinking/feeling) in shared language activities guided by the teacher and with increasing independence.

b. Use simple verb tenses appropriate for the text type and discipline to convey time (e.g., simple past for recounting an experience) in shared language activities guided by the teacher and with increasing independence.

1 a. Use frequently used verbs (e.g., *go, eat, run*) and verb types (e.g., doing, saying, being/having, thinking/feeling) in shared language activities guided by the teacher and sometimes independently.

b. Use simple verb tenses appropriate for the text type and discipline to convey time (e.g., simple past for recounting an experience) in shared language activities guided by the teacher and sometimes independently.

2 a. Use frequently used verbs (e.g., *go, eat, run*) and verb types (e.g., doing, saying, being/having, thinking/feeling) in shared language activities guided by the teacher and sometimes independently.

b. Use simple verb tenses appropriate for the text type and discipline to convey time (e.g., simple past for recounting an experience) in shared language activities guided by the teacher and sometimes independently.

Expanding

K a. Use *a growing number of* verbs and verb types (e.g., doing, saying, being/having, thinking/feeling) in shared language activities guided by the teacher and *independently*.

b. Use *a growing number of* verb tenses appropriate for the text type and discipline to convey time (e.g., *simple past tense for retelling, simple present for a science description*) in shared language activities guided by the teacher and *independently*.

1 a. Use *a growing number of* verbs and verb types (e.g., doing, saying, being/having, thinking/feeling) in shared language activities guided by the teacher and *with increasing independence*.

b. Use *a growing number of* verb tenses appropriate for the text type and discipline to convey time (e.g., *simple past tense for retelling, simple present for a science description*) in shared language activities guided by the teacher and *with increasing independence*.

2 a. Use *a growing number of* verbs and verb types (e.g., doing, saying, being/having)

b. Use a growing number of verb tenses appropriate for the text type and discipline to convey time (e.g., *simple past tense for retelling, simple present for a science description*) in shared language activities guided by the teacher and with *increasing independence*.

Bridging

K a. Use *a wide variety of* verbs and verb types (e.g., doing, saying, being/having, thinking/feeling) in shared language activities guided by the teacher and *independently*.

b. Use *a wide variety of* verb tenses appropriate for the text type and discipline to convey time (e.g., simple present for a science description, *simple future to predict*) in shared language activities guided by the teacher and *independently*.

1 a. Use *a wide variety of* verbs and verb types (e.g., doing, saying, being/having, thinking/feeling) in shared language activities guided by the teacher and *independently*.

b. Use *a wide variety of* verb tenses appropriate for the text type and discipline to convey time (e.g., simple present for a science description, *simple future to predict*) in shared language activities guided by the teacher and *independently*.

2 a. Use *a wide variety of* verbs and verb types (e.g., doing, saying, being/having, thinking/feeling) *independently*.

b. Use *a wide variety of* verb tenses appropriate for the text type and discipline to convey time (e.g., simple present for a science description, simple future to predict) in shared language activities guided by the teacher and *independently*.

Script *in bold italics* indicates content not found in earlier proficiency levels of the same ELD Standard.

Source: *California English Language Development Standards for Grades K–12*, California Department of Education (2012).

What the **Student** Does

Emerging	Expanding	Bridging
Gist: Students use frequently used verbs and verb types in shared language activities guided by the teacher and with some independence. Students use simple verb tenses appropriate for the text type and discipline to show time in shared language activities guided by the teacher and with some independence.		
K They consider:	**K** They *also* consider:	**K** They *also* consider:
• Can I use frequently used verbs appropriately? • Do I use verb types correctly (doing, saying, being/having, thinking/feeling)? • Can I use simple verb tenses (simple past) when I work with the teacher or by myself?	• Can I use simple verb tenses (simple present) when I work with the teacher or by myself?	• Can I use simple verb tenses (simple future) when I work with the teacher or by myself?
Gist: Students use a variety of verbs and verb types in shared language activities guided by the teacher and with some independence. Students use simple verb tenses appropriate for the text type and discipline to show past, present, and future in shared language activities guided by the teacher and with increasing independence.		
1 They consider:	**1** They *also* consider:	**1** They *also* consider:
• Can I use frequently used verbs appropriately? • Do I use verb types correctly (doing, saying, being/having, thinking/feeling)? • Can I use verb tenses (simple past) when I work with the teacher or by myself?	• Can I use verb tenses (simple present) when I work with the teacher or by myself?	• Can I use simple verb tenses (simple future) when I work with the teacher or by myself?
Gist: Students use a variety of verbs and verb types in shared language activities guided by the teacher and with some independence. Students use simple verb tenses appropriate for the text type and discipline to show past, present, and future independently.		
2 They consider:	**2** They *also* consider:	**2** They *also* consider:
• Can I use frequently used verbs appropriately? • Do I use verb types correctly (doing, saying, being/having, thinking/feeling)? • Can I use verb tenses (simple past) when I work with the teacher or by myself?	• Can I use verb tenses (simple present) when I work independently?	• Can I use simple verb tenses (simple future) when I work independently?

Source: California English Language Development Standards for Grades K–12 (2012).

Speaking and Listening Standards	Language Standards
K **SL.K.6:** Speak audibly and express thoughts, feelings, and ideas clearly.	**K** **L.K.1:** Demonstrate command of the conventions of standard English grammar and usage when writing or speaking. a. Print many upper- and lowercase letters. b. Use frequently occurring nouns and verbs. c. Form regular plural nouns orally by adding /s/ or /es/ (e.g., *dog, dogs; wish, wishes*). d. Understand and use question words (interrogatives) (e.g., *who, what, where, when, why, how*). e. Use the most frequently occurring prepositions (e.g., *to, from, in, out, on, off, for, of, by, with*). f. Produce and expand complete sentences in shared language activities.
	K **L.K.6:** Use words and phrases acquired through conversations, reading and being read to, and responding to texts.
1 **SL.1.6:** Produce complete sentences when appropriate to task and situation. (See grade 1 Language standards 1 and 3 for specific expectations.)	**1** **L.1.1:** Demonstrate command of the conventions of standard English grammar and usage when writing or speaking. a. Print all upper- and lowercase letters. b. Use common, proper, and possessive nouns. c. Use singular and plural nouns with matching verbs in basic sentences (e.g., *He hops; We hop*). d. Use personal (subject, object), possessive, and indefinite pronouns (e.g., *I, me, my; they, them, their; anyone, everything*). e. Use verbs to convey a sense of past, present, and future (e.g., *Yesterday I walked home; Today I walk home; Tomorrow I will walk home*). f. Use frequently occurring adjectives. g. Use frequently occurring conjunctions (e.g., *and, but, or, so, because*). h. Use determiners (e.g., articles, demonstratives). i. Use frequently occurring prepositions (e.g., *during, beyond, toward*). j. Produce and expand complete simple and compound declarative, interrogative, imperative, and exclamatory sentences in response to prompts.

continued

continued from previous

Speaking and Listening Standards	Language Standards
	1 **L.1.6:** Use words and phrases acquired through conversations, reading and being read to, and responding to texts, including using frequently occurring conjunctions to signal simple relationships (e.g., *because*).
2 **SL.2.6:** Produce complete sentences when appropriate to task and situation in order to provide requested detail or clarification. (See grade 2 Language standards 1 and 3 for specific expectations.)	**2** **L.2.1:** Demonstrate command of the conventions of standard English grammar and usage when writing or speaking. a. Use collective nouns (e.g., *group*). b. Form and use frequently occurring irregular plural nouns (e.g., *feet, children, teeth, mice, fish*). c. Use reflexive pronouns (e.g., *myself, ourselves*). d. Form and use the past tense of frequently occurring irregular verbs (e.g., *sat, hid, told*). e. Use adjectives and adverbs, and choose between them depending on what is to be modified. f. Produce, expand, and rearrange complete simple and compound sentences (e.g., *The boy watched the movie; The little boy watched the movie; The action movie was watched by the little boy*). g. Create readable documents with legible print.
	2 **L.2.3:** Use knowledge of language and its conventions when writing, speaking, reading, or listening. a. Compare formal and informal uses of English.
	2 **L.2.6:** Use words and phrases acquired through conversations, reading and being read to, and responding to texts, including using adjectives and adverbs to describe (e.g., *When other kids are happy that makes me happy*).

In addition to the ELA Speaking/Listening and Language standards provided in the chart, Standard 3: Using verbs and verb phrases is also linked to ELA Writing standard K.5, 1.5, and 2.5.

Source: *Common Core State Standards, K–12 English Language Arts* (2010).

What the **Teacher** Does

Part II of the CA ELD Standards and the CA CCSS for ELA/Literacy highlight the importance of developing deep awareness of how English works on multiple levels, including discourse, text, sentence, clause, phrase, and word. This multiplicity requires teachers to think strategically about the types of learning experiences that will support their ELL students at varying English proficiency levels to *build up* and *use* the linguistic resources and content knowledge necessary for participating in academic discourse. While teachers continue to help their ELL students develop the type of English used in social situations and, importantly, allow students to use social English, "imperfect" English, and their primary language as they engage in academic tasks, all of the CA ELD standards in Part I and II are focused on developing ELLs' proficiency in academic English across and within the disciplines (p. 295).

Teachers can assist students with using a variety of verbs and verb types in shared language activities guided by the teacher and with some independence. Students use simple verb tenses appropriate for the text type and discipline to show past, present, and future in shared language activities guided by the teacher and with increasing independence:

- Having students circle and underline simple verb tenses that demonstrate past, present, and future in familiar texts.

- Providing a word bank of simple verb tenses to show past, present, and future, which students can use in their own writing. Book such as, *Nouns and Verbs Have a Field Day* by Robin Pulver, and *Kites Sail High: A Book About Verbs* by Ruth Heller, can assist with introducing verb tenses.

- As a class, jointly reconstruct a familiar text by adding a variety of verbs and verb types to show past, present, and future.

- Using sentence strips or Post-its to have pairs of students expand and revise sentences with a variety of verbs and verb types.

- Using sentence frames with a variety of verbs and verb types to assist students with writing past, present, and future.

Tips for Differentiation by Proficiency Level

- *Emerging*—The teacher can select verb and verb phrases from a book that is being read, such as *doing*, *saying*, *being/having*, *thinking/feeling*, or action verbs such as *chase*, *jump*, *walk*, *turn*, *vanish*. The teacher can then place these verbs on sentence strips, so that jointly they can create verb phrases.

- *Expanding*—The teacher can select verb from an ELL's writing sample, and using a document camera, demonstrate how to revise or extend the sentence using verb phrases.

- *Bridging*—The teacher can ask students to identify verb tenses in a text that is familiar to students. Students can then work in pairs to jointly revise the text using different verb tenses (simple present and/or simple future).

Source: 2014 ELA/ELD Framework, p. 295.

Academic Vocabulary—Key Words and Phrases Related to Standard 3: Using verbs and verb phrases

Shared language activities: Developing understanding within a team or classroom based on language (e.g., spoken, text, body language or visuals) in a way that helps them communicate more effectively. This may be simply explaining to another the meaning of a locally used term, or more extensively it may be a level of engagement and interaction that takes months, possibly years to develop.

Verbs and verb phrases: Words that name actions or states of being: they change form to indicate tense, number, voice, or mood.

Verb tenses: Tell the audience when a person did something or when something existed or happened. In English, there are three main tenses: the present, the past, and the future.

Verb types: Categories for classifying verbs, including doing, saying, being/having, and thinking/feeling.

Source: Taberski & Burke, (2014), *The Common Core Companion: The Standards Decoded, Grades K–2.*

Notes

Example of Practice in Snapshot Related to Standard 3: Using verbs and verb phrases

Vignette 4. 2. Discussing "Doing" Verbs in *Chrysanthemum* Designated ELD Instruction in Grade 2

Mrs. Hernandez explains that there are still a lot of thinking/feeling and being/having verbs in a story, and there are many *saying* verbs because there is a lot of dialogue in stories, but that today, they are mostly focusing on the doing verbs that show what a character is feeling or thinking. She tells them that they may also find examples of saying verbs that do this. For example, an author may write, "she sighed," to show that a character is disappointed or sad.

She writes this on the chart as an example. Mrs. Hernandez tells the children that their next task is to be *language detectives*. She has the students work in groups of three to find other examples in books by Kevin Henkes where he shows how a character is feeling or is thinking by using doing or saying verbs. She gives the triads copies of several Kevin Henkes's books, along with a graphic organizer like the one she used to model the task. For each book, some examples have been written in the left-hand column and a space in the right-hand column for students to write their *translations*.

She tells the students that their task is to find a sentence in the text that they think uses doing verbs to show what a character feels or what a character thinks. Next, the groups of three try to agree on what they will write and record it on the graphic organizer, discussing why the author used the doing verb instead of a being/having or thinking/feeling verb with an adjective. As the students engage in the task, she observes their discussions and provides just-in-time scaffolding when needed. Once the time for the task is up, she calls the students back to the rug to discuss their findings. Mrs. Hernandez asks students to tell her where to place the verbs on the Verb Chart, which she posts in the room along with the Using Verbs to Show and Tell chart, so that children will have models for their own story writing.

Primary CA ELD Standards Addressed (Expanding): ELD.PI.2.1—Contribute to class, group, and partner discussions . . . ; ELD.PI.2.6—Describe ideas, phenomena (e.g., how earthworms eat), and text elements (e.g., setting, events) in greater detail based on understanding of a variety of grade-level texts and viewing of multimedia with moderate support; ELD.PII.2.3—Use a growing number of verb types (e.g., doing, saying, being/having, thinking/feeling) with increasing independence.

The snapshots and vignettes cited above can be found in their entirety at https://www.cde.ca.gov/ci/rl/cf/, *ELA/ELD Framework*, p. 349.

Notes

Emerging

K Expand noun phrases in simple ways (e.g., adding a familiar adjective to describe a noun) in order to enrich the meaning of sentences and add details about ideas, people, things, and so on, in shared language activities guided by the teacher and sometimes independently.

1 Expand noun phrases in simple ways (e.g., adding a familiar adjective to describe a noun) in order to enrich the meaning of sentences and add details about ideas, people, things, and the like, in shared language activities guided by the teacher and sometimes independently.

2 Expand noun phrases in simple ways (e.g., adding a familiar adjective to describe a noun) in order to enrich the meaning of sentences and add details about ideas, people, things, and the like, in shared language activities guided by the teacher and sometimes independently.

Expanding

K Expand noun phrases in a *growing number of* ways (e.g., adding a *newly learned* adjective to a noun) in order to enrich the meaning of sentences and add details about ideas, people, things, and so on, in shared language activities guided by the teacher and *with increasing independence.*

1 Expand noun phrases in a *growing number of* ways (e.g., adding a *newly learned* adjective to a noun) in order to enrich the meaning of sentences and add details about ideas, people, things, and the like, in shared language activities guided by the teacher and *with increasing independence.*

2 Expand noun phrases in a *growing number of* ways (e.g., adding a *newly learned* adjective to a noun) in order to enrich the meaning of sentences and add details about ideas, people, things, and the like, in shared language activities guided by the teacher and *with increasing independence.*

Bridging

K Expand noun phrases in a *wide variety of* ways (e.g., adding a *variety of* adjectives to noun *phrases*) in order to enrich the meaning of *phrases/* sentences and add details about ideas, people, things, and so on, in shared language activities guided by the teacher and *independently.*

1 Expand noun phrases in a *wide variety of* ways (e.g., adding a *variety of* adjectives to noun *phrases*) in order to enrich the meaning of *phrases/* sentences and add details about ideas, people, things, and the like, in shared language activities guided by the teacher and *independently.*

2 Expand noun phrases in a *wide variety of* ways (e.g., adding *comparative/superlative* adjectives to nouns) in order to enrich the meaning of *phrases/* sentences and add details about ideas, people, things, and the like, *independently.*

Script *in bold italics* indicates content not found in earlier proficiency levels of the same ELD Standard.

Source: *California English Language Development Standards for Grades K–12*, California Department of Education (November 2012).

What the **Student** Does

Emerging	Expanding	Bridging

Gist: *Students expand noun phrases in simple ways in order to enrich the meaning of sentences and add details in shared language activities guided by the teacher and with some independence.*

K They consider:

- Can I expand nouns and noun phrases by adding familiar adjectives to nouns?
- Can I add details to ideas, people, and things to enrich their meaning?
- Can I expand nouns and noun phrases when I work with the teacher or by myself?

K They *also* consider:

- Can I expand nouns and noun phrases by adding newly learned adjectives to nouns?

K They *also* consider:

- Can I expand nouns and noun phrases by adding a variety of adjectives to nouns?
- Can I expand nouns and noun phrases when I work by myself?

Gist: *Students expand noun phrases in a variety of ways in order to enrich the meaning of sentences and add details in shared language activities guided by the teacher and with increasing independence*

1 They consider:

- Can I expand nouns and noun phrases by adding familiar adjectives to nouns?
- Can I add details to ideas, people, and things to enrich their meaning?
- Can I expand nouns and noun phrases when I work with the teacher or by myself?

1 They *also* consider:

- Can I expand nouns and noun phrases by adding newly learned adjectives to nouns?

1 They *also* consider:

- Can I expand nouns and noun phrases by adding a variety of adjectives to nouns?
- Can I expand nouns and noun phrases when I work by myself?

Gist: *Students expand noun phrases in a variety of ways in order to enrich the meaning of sentences and add details independently.*

2 They consider:

- Can I expand nouns and noun phrases by adding familiar adjectives to nouns?
- Can I add details to ideas, people, and things to enrich their meaning?
- Can I expand nouns and noun phrases when I work with the teacher or by myself?

2 They *also* consider:

- Can I expand nouns and noun phrases by adding newly learned adjectives to nouns?

2 They *also* consider:

- Can I expand nouns and noun phrases by adding comparative/superlative adjectives to nouns?
- Can I expand nouns and noun phrases when I work by myself?

Speaking and Listening Standards	Language Standards
K SL.K.6: Speak audibly and express thoughts, feelings, and ideas clearly.	**K L.K.1:** Demonstrate command of the conventions of standard English grammar and usage when writing or speaking. a. Print many upper- and lowercase letters. b. Use frequently occurring nouns and verbs. c. Form regular plural nouns orally by adding /s/ or /es/ (e.g., *dog, dogs; wish, wishes*). d. Understand and use question words (interrogatives) (e.g., *who, what, where, when, why, how*). e. Use the most frequently occurring prepositions (e.g., *to, from, in, out, on, off, for, of, by, with*). f. Produce and expand complete sentences in shared language activities.
	K L.K.6: Use words and phrases acquired through conversations, reading and being read to, and responding to texts.
1 SL.1.6: Produce complete sentences when appropriate to task and situation. (See grade 1 Language standards 1 and 3 for specific expectations.)	**1 L.1.1:** Demonstrate command of the conventions of standard English grammar and usage when writing or speaking. a. Print all upper- and lowercase letters. b. Use common, proper, and possessive nouns. c. Use singular and plural nouns with matching verbs in basic sentences (e.g., *He hops; We hop*). d. Use personal (subject, object), possessive, and indefinite pronouns (e.g., *I, me, my; they, them, their; anyone, everything*). e. Use verbs to convey a sense of past, present, and future (e.g., *Yesterday I walked home; Today I walk home; Tomorrow I will walk home*). f. Use frequently occurring adjectives. g. Use frequently occurring conjunctions (e.g., *and, but, or, so, because*). h. Use determiners (e.g., articles, demonstratives). i. Use frequently occurring prepositions (e.g., *during, beyond, toward*). j. Produce and expand complete simple and compound declarative, interrogative, imperative, and exclamatory sentences in response to prompts.

continued

continued from previous

Speaking and Listening Standards	Language Standards
	1 **L.1.6:** Use words and phrases acquired through conversations, reading and being read to, and responding to texts, including using frequently occurring conjunctions to signal simple relationships (e.g., *because*).
2 **SL.2.6:** Produce complete sentences when appropriate to task and situation in order to provide requested detail or clarification. (See grade 2 Language standards 1 and 3 for specific expectations.)	**2** **L.2.1:** Demonstrate command of the conventions of standard English grammar and usage when writing or speaking. a. Use collective nouns (e.g., *group*). b. Form and use frequently occurring irregular plural nouns (e.g., *feet, children, teeth, mice, fish*). c. Use reflexive pronouns (e.g., *myself, ourselves*). d. Form and use the past tense of frequently occurring irregular verbs (e.g., *sat, hid, told*). e. Use adjectives and adverbs, and choose between them depending on what is to be modified. f. Produce, expand, and rearrange complete simple and compound sentences (e.g., *The boy watched the movie; The little boy watched the movie; The action movie was watched by the little boy*). g. Create readable documents with legible print.
	2 **L.2.3:** Use knowledge of language and its conventions when writing, speaking, reading, or listening. a. Compare formal and informal uses of English.
	2 **L.2.6:** Use words and phrases acquired through conversations, reading and being read to, and responding to texts, including using adjectives and adverbs to describe (e.g., *When other kids are happy that makes me happy*).

In addition to the ELA Language and Speaking/Listening standards provided on this chart, ELD Standard 4: Using nouns and noun phrases is **also** correlated with ELA Writing standards K.5, 1.5, and 2.5.

Source: *Common Core State Standards, K–12 English Language Arts* (2010).

What the **Teacher** Does

Part II, "Learning About How English Works," focuses on developing children's abilities to use the language resources English affords for different purposes and contexts. Students learn how language is used to create different text types (e.g., how a story is typically organized sequentially with predictable stages, how an opinion piece is organized around a stated point of view and explained with reasons and information), how descriptive vocabulary or prepositional phrases can enrich and expand their ideas (e.g., *I like pizza.* → *Pizza is scrumptious.*), and how language can be used to combine or condense their ideas in particular ways (e.g., *She's a doctor. She's amazing. She saved the animals.* → *She's the amazing doctor who saved the animals.*) (p. 142).

Teachers can assist students with expanding noun phrases in a variety of ways in order to enrich the meaning of sentences and add details in shared language activities guided by the teacher and with increasing independence:

- Using sentence strips to model building or expanding sentences by adding newly learned adjectives to nouns, and then analyze and discuss how this changed or enhanced the meaning.

- Selecting familiar texts and underline and circle noun phrases and then discuss how they have been expanded.

- Rewriting familiar texts as a class or small group, in order to expand sentences, and then discuss how the meaning has changed or been enhanced.

- Having students rewrite their own sentences, by adding noun phrases, in order to expand or change meaning.

- For more complexity, teachers can model building or expanding sentences by adding superlatives or comparative adjectives to nouns or noun phrases by using sentence strips.

Tips for Differentiation by Proficiency Level

- *Emerging*—At the emerging level, teachers can use sentence strips to model how a noun and noun phrase can be expanded by adding familiar adjectives to a text that has been read aloud to students several times.

- *Expanding*—At the expanding level, teachers can highlight how a noun and noun phrase can be expanded by adding familiar adjectives to a recognizable text.

- *Bridging*—At the bridging level, teachers can provide students with Post-its or individual sentence strips, so that they can practice expanding noun and noun phrases using adjectives that have introduced.

Source: 2014 ELA/ELD Framework, p. 142.

Academic Vocabulary—Key Words and Phrases Related to Standard 4: Using nouns and noun phrases

Expand nouns and noun phrases: Using adjectives to add detail to the descriptions of nouns, in order to add meaning to sentences.

Nouns and noun phrases: Words or group of words that function in a sentence as subject, object, or prepositional object, usually naming persons, places, things, and feelings.

Shared language activities: Developing understanding within a team or classroom based on language (e.g., spoken, text, body language or visuals) in a way that helps them communicate more effectively. This may be simply explaining to another the meaning of a locally used term, or more extensively it may be a level of engagement and interaction that takes months, possibly years to develop.

Using comparatives and superlatives: Making comparisons about nouns. Comparative adjectives compare two nouns, usually by adding *er* to the adjective. *She is taller than her brother.* Superlative adjectives compare three or more nouns, usually by adding *est* to the adjective. *She is the tallest of all five children.*

Source: Taberski & Burke, (2014), *The Common Core Companion: The Standards Decoded, Grades K–2.*

Notes

Example of Practice in Snapshot Related to Standard 4: Using nouns and noun phrases

Vignette 3.2. Retelling *The Three Little Pigs* Using Past Tense Verbs and Expanded Sentences Designated ELD Instruction in Transitional Kindergarten

In ELA instruction, Ms. Campbell has just guided her students to rewrite, or jointly reconstruct, the story of *The Three Little Pigs* (see Vignette 3.1). As she observed students during their oral retellings of the story in English, she noticed that ELLs at the Emerging level of English language proficiency were not consistently using past tense verbs or expanding their sentences with much detail. She would like the children to feel more confident orally retelling stories in general and using past tense verb forms and particular language resources to expand and enrich their sentences, so she plans to focus on these two areas in her designated ELD lessons this week.

CA CCSS for ELA/Literacy: RL.K.2—With prompting and support, retell familiar stories, including key details; SL.K.2—Confirm understanding of a text read aloud . . . ; W.K.3—Use a combination of drawing, dictating, and writing to narrate a single event or several loosely linked events, tell about the events in the order in which they occurred . . . ; L.K.6—Use words and phrases acquired through conversations, reading and being read to, and responding to texts.

CA ELD Standards (Expanding): ELD.PI.K.12a—Retell texts and recount experiences using complete sentences and key words; ELD.PII.K.1—Apply understanding of how different text types are organized to express ideas (e.g., how a story is organized sequentially with predictable stages . . .); ELD.PII.K.2—Apply understanding of how ideas, events, or reasons are linked throughout a text using a growing number of connecting words or phrases (e.g., next, after a long time) . . .

The snapshots and vignettes cited above can be found in their entirety at https://www.cde.ca.gov/ci/rl/cf/, *ELA/ELD Framework*, p. 196.

Notes

Notes

Emerging

K Expand sentences with frequently used prepositional phrases (such as *in the house, on the boat*) to provide details (e.g., time, manner, place, cause) about a familiar activity or process in shared language activities guided by the teacher and sometimes independently.

1 Expand sentences with frequently used prepositional phrases (such as *in the house, on the boat*) to provide details (e.g., time, manner, place, cause) about a familiar activity or process in shared language activities guided by the teacher and sometimes independently.

2 Expand sentences with frequently used adverbials (e.g., prepositional phrases such as, *at school, with my friend*) to provide details (e.g., time, manner, place, cause) about a familiar activity or process in shared language activities guided by the teacher and sometimes independently.

Expanding

K Expand sentences with prepositional phrases to provide details (e.g., time, manner, place, cause) about a familiar *or new* activity or process in shared language activities guided by the teacher and *with increasing independence.*

1 Expand sentences with prepositional phrases to provide details (e.g., time, manner, place, cause) about a familiar *or new* activity or process in shared language activities guided by the teacher and *with increasing independence.*

2 Expand sentences with a *growing number of* adverbials (e.g., *adverbs*, prepositional phrases) to provide details (e.g., time, manner, place, cause) about a familiar *or new* activity *with increasing independence.*

Bridging

K Expand *simple and compound sentences* with prepositional phrases to provide details (e.g., time, manner, place, cause) in shared language activities guided by the teacher and *independently.*

1 Expand *simple and compound sentences* with prepositional phrases to provide details (e.g., time, manner, place, cause) in shared language activities guided by the teacher and *independently.*

2 Expand sentences with a *variety of* adverbials (e.g., adverbs, *adverb phrases*, prepositional phrases) to provide details (e.g., time, manner, place, cause) *independently.*

Script *in bold italics* indicates content not found in earlier proficiency levels of the same ELD Standard.

Source: *California English Language Development Standards for Grades K–12*, California Department of Education (2012).

What the **Student** Does

Emerging	Expanding	Bridging

Gist: Students expand sentences with prepositional phrases to provide details about a familiar activity in shared language activities guided by the teacher and with some independence.

K They consider:

- Can I expand my sentences by adding details about familiar activities?
- Can I add details about time, manner, place, or cause?
- Can I expand my sentences when I work with the teacher or by myself?

K They *also* consider:

- Can I expand my sentences by adding details about new activities or processes?

K They *also* consider:

- Can I expand both simple and compound sentences?
- Can I expand sentences when I work by myself?

Gist: Students expand sentences with prepositional phrases to provide details about a new activity in shared language activities guided by the teacher and with increasing independence.

1 They consider:

- Can I expand my sentences by adding details about familiar activities?
- Can I add details about time, manner, place, or cause?
- Can I expand my sentences when I work with the teacher or by myself?

1 They *also* consider:

- Can I expand my sentences by adding details about new activities or processes?

1 They *also* consider:

- Can I expand both simple and compound sentences?
- Can I expand sentences when I work by myself?

Gist: Students expand sentences with adverbials to provide details about a familiar or new activity or process independently.

2 They consider:

- Can I expand my sentences by adding frequently used adverbials?
- Can I add details about time, manner, place, or cause?
- Can I expand my sentences when I work with the teacher or by myself?

2 They *also* consider:

- Can I expand my sentences by adding a growing number of adverbials?

2 They *also* consider:

- Can I expand my sentences by adding a variety of adverbials?
- Can I expand sentences when I work by myself?

Source: *California English Language Development Standards for Grades K–12* (2012).

Speaking and Listening Standards	Language Standards
K **SL.K.4:** Describe familiar people, places, things, and events and, with prompting and support, provide additional detail.	**K** **L.K.1:** Demonstrate command of the conventions of standard English grammar and usage when writing or speaking. a. Print many upper- and lowercase letters. b. Use frequently occurring nouns and verbs. c. Form regular plural nouns orally by adding /s/ or /es/ (e.g., *dog, dogs; wish, wishes*). d. Understand and use question words (interrogatives) (e.g., *who, what, where, when, why, how*). e. Use the most frequently occurring prepositions (e.g., *to, from, in, out, on, off, for, of, by, with*). f. Produce and expand complete sentences in shared language activities.
	K **L.K.6:** Use words and phrases acquired through conversations, reading and being read to, and responding to texts.
1 **SL.1.4:** Describe people, places, things, and events with relevant details, expressing ideas and feelings clearly. a. Memorize and recite poems, rhymes, and songs with expression.	**1** **L.1.1:** Demonstrate command of the conventions of standard English grammar and usage when writing or speaking. a. Print all upper- and lowercase letters. b. Use common, proper, and possessive nouns. c. Use singular and plural nouns with matching verbs in basic sentences (e.g., *He hops; We hop*). d. Use personal (subject, object), possessive, and indefinite pronouns (e.g., *I, me, my; they, them, their; anyone, everything*). e. Use verbs to convey a sense of past, present, and future (e.g., *Yesterday I walked home; Today I walk home; Tomorrow I will walk home*). f. Use frequently occurring adjectives. g. Use frequently occurring conjunctions (e.g., *and, but, or, so, because*). h. Use determiners (e.g., articles, demonstratives). i. Use frequently occurring prepositions (e.g., *during, beyond, toward*). j. Produce and expand complete simple and compound declarative, interrogative, imperative, and exclamatory sentences in response to prompts.

continued

continued from previous

Speaking and Listening Standards	Language Standards
	1 **L.1.6:** Use words and phrases acquired through conversations, reading and being read to, and responding to texts, including using frequently occurring conjunctions to signal simple relationships (e.g., *because*).
2 **SL.2.4:** Tell a story or recount an experience with appropriate facts and relevant, descriptive details, speaking audibly in coherent sentences. a. Plan and deliver a narrative presentation that: recounts a well-elaborated event, includes details, reflects a logical sequence, and provides a conclusion.	**2** **L.2.1:** Demonstrate command of the conventions of standard English grammar and usage when writing or speaking. a. Use collective nouns (e.g., *group*). b. Form and use frequently occurring irregular plural nouns (e.g., *feet, children, teeth, mice, fish*). c. Use reflexive pronouns (e.g., *myself, ourselves*). d. Form and use the past tense of frequently occurring irregular verbs (e.g., *sat, hid, told*). e. Use adjectives and adverbs, and choose between them depending on what is to be modified. f. Produce, expand, and rearrange complete simple and compound sentences (e.g., *The boy watched the movie; The little boy watched the movie; The action movie was watched by the little boy*). g. Create readable documents with legible print.
	2 **L.2.3:** Use knowledge of language and its conventions when writing, speaking, reading, or listening. a. Compare formal and informal uses of English.
	2 **L.2.6:** Use words and phrases acquired through conversations, reading and being read to, and responding to texts, including using adjectives and adverbs to describe (e.g., *When other kids are happy that makes me happy*).

In addition to the ELA Speaking/Listening and Language standards provided in the chart, Standard 5: Modifying to add details is also linked to ELA Writing standard K.5, 1.5, and 2.5.

Source: *Common Core State Standards, K–12 English Language Arts* (2010).

What the **Teacher** Does

Part II, "Learning About How English Works," focuses on developing children's abilities to use the language resources English affords for different purposes and contexts. Students learn how language is used to create different text types (e.g., how a story is typically organized sequentially with predictable stages, how an opinion piece is organized around a stated point of view and explained with reasons and information), how descriptive vocabulary or prepositional phrases can enrich and expand their ideas (e.g., *I like pizza.* → *Pizza is scrumptious.*), and how language can be used to combine or condense their ideas in particular ways (e.g., *She's a doctor. She's amazing. She saved the animals.* → *She's the amazing doctor who saved the animals.*) (p. 142).

Teachers can assist students with expanding sentences with prepositional phrases to provide details about a new activity in shared language activities guided by the teacher and with increasing independence:

- Conducting think alouds, which can provide a model for how students can take an idea and use details from a text to expand their responses.

- Using sentence strips to have students expand and manipulate sentences using prepositional phrases to provide details. Prepositional phrases should be taught by category: location, time, manner, or cause. For example, prepositional phrases associated with time can include *before recess, during the game, after lunch, in the morning, at night, on Saturday.*

- Using familiar texts and having students underline and circle prepositional phrases and details, and then apply those to their own writing.

- Rewriting familiar texts using prepositional phrases previously taught in order to expand sentences.

- Rewriting students' own sentences by adding additional details from a word bank of prepositional phrases.

Tips for Differentiation by Proficiency Level

- *Emerging*—At the emerging level, teachers can use sentence frames to show students how they can add details to simple sentences. For example, "*The most important part of the story is _____ because _____ and _____.*" Along with the sentence frame, teachers can model locating details from a text to extend their thoughts.

- *Expanding*—At the expanding level, teachers can use sentence strips to demonstrate how to add details to basic sentences.

- *Bridging*—At the bridging level, teachers can place students' own brief sentences on the board and discuss with the class how they can extend their thoughts, using details from the text that was connected to the original sentences.

Source: 2014 ELA/ELD Framework, p. 142.

Academic Vocabulary—Key Words and Phrases Related to Standard 5: Modifying to add details

Adverbs and adverbials: Using words (an adverb) or a group of words (an adverbial phrase or an adverbial clause) that modifies or more closely defines the sentence or the verb.

Expand sentences: Using adjectives, prepositional phrases, and other adverbials to add detail to sentences.

Prepositional phrases: Using a preposition and its object (e.g., *at my house*) to add detail to sentences.

Shared language activities: Developing understanding within a team or classroom based on language (e.g., spoken, text, body language or visuals) in a way that helps them communicate more effectively. This may be simply explaining to another the meaning of a locally used term, or more extensively, it may be a level of engagement and interaction that takes months, possibly years to develop.

Simple and compound sentences: Simple sentences contain only one subject and a predicate, but a compound sentence contains more than one subject and more than one predicate.

Verbs and verb phrases: Words or group of words that function in a sentence as actions, conditions, or states or being. A verb phrase may contain the verb, the helping verb, and any direct or indirect objects.

Source: Taberski & Burke, (2014), *The Common Core Companion: The Standards Decoded, Grades K–2.*

Notes

Example of Practice in Snapshot Related to Standard 5: Modifying to add details

---

Snapshot 3.11. Expanding Sentences and Building Vocabulary Designated ELD Connected to ELA/Social Studies in Grade 1

Because Mr. Dupont's ELL children are at the Bridging level of English language proficiency, during designated ELD he provides his students with extended opportunities to discuss their ideas and opinions, as he knows that this will support them later when writing down their ideas. He strategically targets particular language that he would like students to use in their opinion pieces by constructing sentence frames that contain specific vocabulary and grammatical structures that will enable his students to be more precise and detailed (e.g., "*My favorite hero is* _____ *because* _____. _____ *was* very courageous *when* _____."). He explains to the children how they can expand their ideas in different ways by adding information about where, when, how, and so forth. For example, he explains that instead of simply saying, "*She worked on a farm*," children could say, "*She worked on a farm* in California," or they could add even more detail and precision by saying, "*She worked on a farm* in the central valley of California." He provides his students with many opportunities to construct these expanded sentence structures as the students discuss the historical figures they are learning about and then write short summaries of their discussions at the end of each lesson. During these lessons, he encourages the children to refer to the texts they have previously read together and to cite evidence from them to support their ideas.

CA ELD Standards (Bridging): ELD.PI.K–1.1, 3, 6, 10, 12b; ELD.PII.K–1.4–5, 6

CA CCSS for ELA/Literacy: RI.1.1; SL.1.1, 4, 6; L.1.6

The snapshots and vignettes cited above can be found in their entirety at https://www.cde.ca.gov/ci/rl/cf/, *ELA/ELD Framework*, p. 260.

Notes

_____

_____

_____

_____

_____

_____

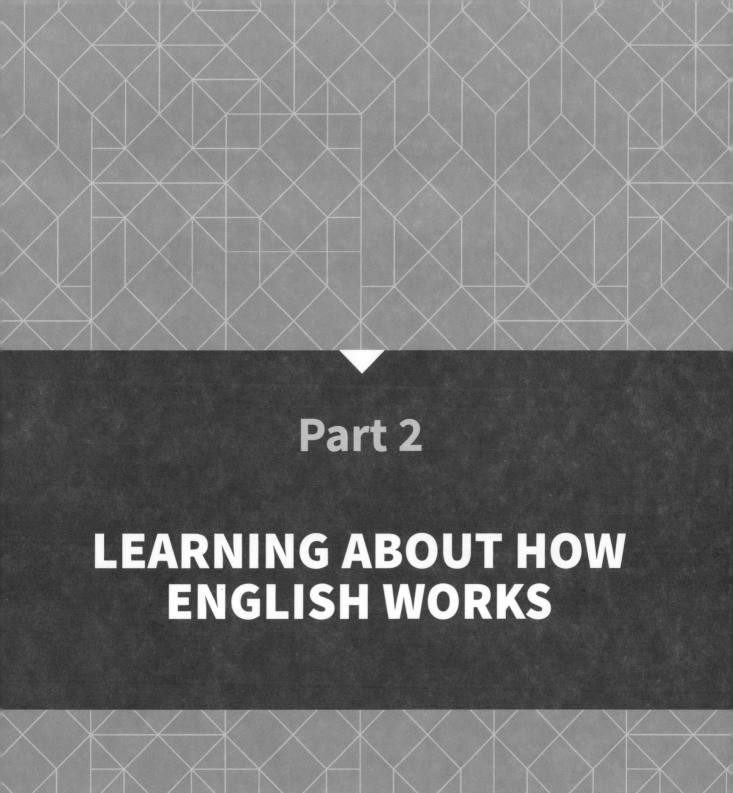

Part 2

LEARNING ABOUT HOW ENGLISH WORKS

C *Connecting and Condensing Ideas*

Introduction

Part II of the *California ELD Standards* promotes English Language Learners' abilities to *learn about how English works* so that they acquire knowledge about English and their abilities to use English to be successful in school. Part II **comes second in the standards** so that ELLs can use their awareness of how English works to make meaning, comprehend, and produce language in various ways and in a range of content areas. Part II, Learning About How English Works, is organized into the following ways of using language meaningfully:

A. Structuring Cohesive Texts

- *Understanding text structure and organization* based on purpose, text type, and discipline
- *Understanding cohesion* and how language resources across a text contribute to the way a text unfolds and flows

B. Expanding and Enriching Ideas

- *Using verbs and verb phrases* to create precision and clarity in different text types
- *Using nouns and noun phrases* to expand ideas and provide more detail
- *Modifying to add details* to provide more information and create precision

C. Connecting and Condensing Ideas

- *Connecting ideas* within sentences by combining clauses
- *Condensing ideas* within sentences using a variety of language resources

Cluster C. Connecting and Condensing Ideas within sentences by combining clauses and using a variety of language resources have the same general descriptions K–12 for the two standards in the cluster. These include

1. *Connecting ideas* within sentences by combining clauses—ELLs can be taught how to combine clauses to make connections between and join ideas in shared activities guided by the teacher. Teachers can model how to create compound sentences with *and, but,* or *so.* Students can also be taught how to express cause and effect, and rearrange complex sentences.

2. *Condensing ideas* within sentences using a variety of language resources—Students can be taught to condense dense texts by using nominalization, which is when a verb is transformed into a noun or noun phrase (e.g., develop to development or grow to growth). By turning actions into things, nominalization allows readers and writers to create abstractions, condense entire events, theories, and concepts into nouns and noun phrases, as well as to create relationships between abstractions, arguments, or evaluations (ELA/ELD Framework Appendix B, 2012, p. 14).

In this document, the section on What the Student Does provides specific descriptions of competence with each of the Connecting and Condensing Ideas standards at the appropriate grade range and proficiency level. Similarly, the section on What the Teacher Does provides specific strategies for developing competence with each of the Connecting and Condensing Ideas standards at the appropriate grade range.

Source: *California English Language Development Standards, K–12* (2012). Appendix B, "The California English Language Development Standards Part II: Learning About How English Works," provides an excellent summary of the research used in developing Part II of the standards.

Emerging

K Combine clauses in a few basic ways to make connections between and join ideas (e.g., creating compound sentences, using *and, but, so*) in shared language activities guided by the teacher and sometimes independently.

1 Combine clauses in a few basic ways to make connections between and join ideas (e.g., creating compound sentences, using *and, but, so*) in shared language activities guided by the teacher and sometimes independently.

2 Combine clauses in a few basic ways to make connections between and to join ideas (e.g., creating compound sentences, using *and, but, so*) in shared language activities guided by the teacher and sometimes independently.

Expanding

K Combine clauses *in an increasing variety of ways* to make connections between and join ideas, for example, *to express cause/effect (e.g., She jumped because the dog barked)* in shared language activities guided by the teacher and *with increasing independence.*

1 Combine clauses *in an increasing variety of ways* to make connections between and join ideas, for example, *to express cause/effect (e.g., She jumped because the dog barked)* in shared language activities guided by the teacher and *with increasing independence.*

2 Combine clauses *in an increasing variety of ways* to make connections between and to join ideas, for example, *to express cause/effect (e.g., She jumped because the dog barked)* in shared language activities guided by the teacher and *with increasing independence.*

Bridging

K Combine clauses *in a wide* variety of ways (e.g., *rearranging complete simple sentences to form compound sentences*) to make connections between and join ideas, (*e.g., The boy was hungry. The boy ate a sandwich – The boy was hungry so he ate a sandwich.*) in shared language activities guided by the teacher and *independently.*

1 Combine clauses *in a wide* variety of ways (e.g., *rearranging complete simple sentences to form compound sentences*) to make connections between and join ideas, (*e.g., The boy was hungry. The boy ate a sandwich – The boy was hungry so he ate a sandwich.*) in shared language activities guided by the teacher and *independently.*

2 Combine clauses *in a wide* variety of ways (e.g., *rearranging complete simple sentences to form compound sentences*) to make connections between and to join ideas (*e.g., The boy was hungry. The boy ate a sandwich – The boy was hungry so he ate a sandwich.*) in shared language activities guided by the teacher and *independently.*

Script *in bold italics* indicates content not found in earlier proficiency levels of the same ELD Standard.

Source: *California English Language Development Standards for Grades K–12*, California Department of Education (2012).

What the **Student** Does

Emerging	Expanding	Bridging

Gist: Students combine clauses in a few basic ways to make connections and join ideas in shared language activities guided by the teacher and with some independence.

K They consider:

- Can I combine clauses to make connections and join ideas?
- Can I form compound sentences?
- Can I connect ideas when I work with the teacher or by myself?

K They *also* consider:

- Can I combine clauses in order to show cause and effect?

K They *also* consider:

- Can I rearrange simple sentences into compound sentences?
- Can I connect ideas when I work by myself?

Gist: Students combine clauses in a variety of ways to make connections and join ideas in shared language activities guided by the teacher and with increasing independence.

1 They consider:

- Can I combine clauses to make connections and join ideas?
- Can I form compound sentences?
- Can I connect ideas when I work with the teacher or by myself?

1 They *also* consider:

- Can I combine clauses in order to show cause and effect?

1 They *also* consider:

- Can I rearrange simple sentences into compound sentences?
- Can I connect ideas when I work by myself?

Gist: Students combine clauses in a wide variety of ways to make connections and join ideas independently.

2 They consider:

- Can I combine clauses to make connections and join ideas?
- Can I form compound sentences?
- Can I connect ideas when I work with the teacher or by myself?

2 They *also* consider:

- Can I combine clauses in order to show cause and effect?

2 They *also* consider:

- Can I rearrange simple sentences into compound sentences?
- Can I connect ideas when I work by myself?

Source: California English Language Development Standards for Grades K–12 (2012).

Speaking and Listening Standards	Language Standards
K SL.K.4: Describe familiar people, places, things, and events and, with prompting and support, provide additional detail.	**K L.K.1:** Demonstrate command of the conventions of standard English grammar and usage when writing or speaking. a. Print many upper- and lowercase letters. b. Use frequently occurring nouns and verbs. c. Form regular plural nouns orally by adding /s/ or /es/ (e.g., *dog, dogs; wish, wishes*). d. Understand and use question words (interrogatives) (e.g., *who, what, where, when, why, how*). e. Use the most frequently occurring prepositions (e.g., *to, from, in, out, on, off, for, of, by, with*). f. Produce and expand complete sentences in shared language activities.
K SL.K.6: Speak audibly and express thoughts, feelings, and ideas clearly.	**K L.K.6:** Use words and phrases acquired through conversations, reading and being read to, and responding to texts.
1 SL.1.4: Describe people, places, things, and events with relevant details, expressing ideas and feelings clearly. a. Memorize and recide poems, rhymes, and songs with expression.	**1 L.1.1:** Demonstrate command of the conventions of standard English grammar and usage when writing or speaking. a. Print all upper- and lowercase letters. b. Use common, proper, and possessive nouns. c. Use singular and plural nouns with matching verbs in basic sentences (e.g., *He hops; We hop*). d. Use personal (subject, object), possessive, and indefinite pronouns (e.g., *I, me, my; they, them, their; anyone, everything*). e. Use verbs to convey a sense of past, present, and future (e.g., *Yesterday I walked home; Today I walk home; Tomorrow I will walk home*). f. Use frequently occurring adjectives. g. Use frequently occurring conjunctions (e.g., *and, but, or, so, because*). h. Use determiners (e.g., articles, demonstratives). i. Use frequently occurring prepositions (e.g., *during, beyond, toward*). j. Produce and expand complete simple and compound declarative, interrogative, imperative, and exclamatory sentences in response to prompts.

continued

continued from previous

Speaking and Listening Standards	**Language Standards**
1 **SL.1.6:** Produce complete sentences when appropriate to task and situation. (See grade 1 Language standards 1 and 3 for specific expectations.)	**1** **L.1.6:** Use words and phrases acquired through conversations, reading and being read to, and responding to texts, including using frequently occurring conjunctions to signal simple relationships (e.g., *because*).
2 **SL.2.1:** Participate in collaborative conversations with diverse partners about *grade 2 topics and texts* with peers and adults in small and larger groups. a. Follow agreed-upon rules for discussions (e.g., gaining the floor in respectful ways listening to others with care, speaking one at a time about the topics and texts under discussion). b. Build on others' talk in conversations by linking their comments to the remarks of others. c. Ask for clarification and further explanation as needed about the topics and texts under discussion.	**2** **L.2.1:** Demonstrate command of the conventions of standard English grammar and usage when writing or speaking. a. Use collective nouns (e.g., *group*). b. Form and use frequently occurring irregular plural nouns (e.g., *feet, children, teeth, mice, fish*). c. Use reflexive pronouns (e.g., *myself, ourselves*). d. Form and use the past tense of frequently occurring irregular verbs (e.g., *sat, hid, told*). e. Use adjectives and adverbs, and choose between them depending on what is to be modified. f. Produce, expand, and rearrange complete simple and compound sentences (e.g., *The boy watched the movie; The little boy watched the movie; The action movie was watched by the little boy*). g. Create readable documents with legible print.
2 **SL.2.3:** Ask and answer questions about what a speaker says in order to clarify comprehension, gather additional information, or deepen understanding of a topic or issue.	**2** **L.2.3:** Use knowledge of language and its conventions when writing, speaking, reading, or listening. a. Compare formal and informal uses of English.
2 **SL.2.6:** Produce complete sentences when appropriate to task and situation in order to provide requested detail or clarification. (See grade 2 Language standards 1 and 3 for specific expectations.)	**2** **L.2.6:** Use words and phrases acquired through conversations, reading and being read to, and responding to texts, including using adjectives and adverbs to describe (e.g., *When other kids are happy that makes me happy*).

In addition to the ELA Speaking/Listening and Language standards provided in the chart, Standard 6: Connecting ideas is also linked to ELA Writing standard K.1–3, 5, 1.1–3, 5, and 2.1–3, 5.

Source: *Common Core State Standards, K–12 English Language Arts* (2010).

What the **Teacher** Does

Part II of the CA ELD Standards and the CA CCSS for ELA/Literacy highlight the importance of developing deep awareness of how English works on multiple levels, including discourse, text, sentence, clause, phrase, and word. This multiplicity requires teachers to think strategically about the types of learning experiences that will support their ELL students at varying English proficiency levels to *build up* and *use* the linguistic resources and content knowledge necessary for participating in academic discourse. While teachers continue to help their ELL students develop the type of English used in social situations and, importantly, allow students to use social English, "imperfect" English, and their primary language as they engage in academic tasks, all of the CA ELD standards in Part I and II are focused on developing ELLs' proficiency in academic English across and within the disciplines (p. 295).

Teachers can assist students with connecting ideas to combine clauses in a few basic ways to make connections between and join ideas (e.g., creating compound sentences using *and, but, so*) in shared language activities guided by the teacher and sometimes independently:

- Modeling for students how to connect ideas and combine clauses using familiar texts. Teachers can build sentences that make connections between and join ideas on the board or an easel chart.
- Using sentence strips with *and, but,* and *so* printed on them, so that students can combine clauses to make connections between and join ideas.
- Having students work in partners to revise or reconstruct sentences from familiar texts to make connections between and join ideas.
- In partners, combine clauses to demonstrate cause and effect using a familiar text or students' own writing.
- In small groups, rearrange simple sentences from a familiar text into complex sentences. The group that does this fastest and most accurately receives a reward. Students can have several rounds of this for additional practice.
- Explicitly teaching students the seven coordinating conjunctions including—*and, but, for, nor, or, so, yet*—in order to create compound and complex sentences. Have students practice more complex sentences by revising a sentence that they have written using a coordinating conjunction.
- Teaching students that subordinate conjunctions provide a necessary transition between two ideas in a sentence, and that the transition will indicate time, place, or cause-and-effect relationships. Have students identify subordinate conjunctions—such as *once, where,* and *because*—in a familiar text.

Tips for Differentiation by Proficiency Level

- *Emerging*—At the emerging level, teachers can use sentence strips with familiar texts to model how a simple sentence can be rearranged into a complex sentence.
- *Expanding*—At the expanding level, teachers can use students' own writing to model how to rearrange simple sentences into complex sentences. Students can then work in partners to do the same with each other's sentences.
- *Bridging*—At the bridging level, teachers can use a familiar text to demonstrate how an author combined clauses to show cause and effect. Students can then identify cause an effect clauses in the same or other texts.

Source: 2014 ELA/ELD Framework, p. 295.

Academic Vocabulary—Key Words and Phrases Related to Standard 6: Connecting ideas

Cause/effect: Showing a relationship between events or things, where one is the result of the other or others, a combination of action and reaction. For example, *"Because I was so tired, I went to bed."*

Clauses: Using a group of words containing a subject and predicate and functioning as a member of a compound sentence, but is not a sentence by itself. For example, *"When it rains, I put on my galoshes."*

Complex sentences: Complex sentences contain a noun, verb, or adverbial clause. For example, *"This poem, which was translated from Spanish, is still very relevant for English-speaking cultures."*

Compound complex sentences: Compound complex sentences contain a noun, verb, or adverbial clause, combined with a second noun, verb, or adverbial phrase. For example, *"This poem, which was translated from Spanish, is still very relevant for English-speaking cultures, and many poems follow the Spanish patterns."*

Coordinating conjunction: A conjunction placed between words, phrases, clauses, or sentences of equal rank (e.g., *and, but, or*).

Shared language activities: Developing understanding within a team or classroom based on language (e.g., spoken, text, body language, or visuals) in a way that helps them communicate more effectively. This may be simply explaining to another the meaning of a locally used term, or more extensively it may be a level of engagement and interaction that takes months, possibly years to develop.

Simple and compound sentences: Simple sentences contain only one subject and a predicate, but a compound sentence contains more than one subject and more than one predicate.

Subordinating conjunction: A word that connects a main clause to a subordinate clause. A main clause is an independent clause that can stand alone by itself as a sentence. These phrases cannot stand by themselves, and their meaning is dependent upon that of the independent clause.

Source: Taberski & Burke, (2014), *The Common Core Companion: The Standards Decoded, Grades K–2.*

Notes

Example of Practice in Snapshot Related to Standard 6: Connecting ideas

Vignette 3.6. Unpacking Sentences Designated ELD Instruction in Grade 1

Mrs. Fabian thinks aloud; she pulls shorter sentence strips from behind the original sentence and places them in the rows below, visually *unpacking* the meaning of the sentence so that students can see the breakdown. She reads each sentence as she places it in the pocket chart.

Mrs. Fabian:

There's a forager bee.

The bee collects nectar.

The bee has pollen on its legs.

The bee carries the pollen to many flowers.

"Can you see how I unpacked or separated all the ideas in the sentence?"

There are really just two big ideas. The first is that the bee is collecting nectar, and the second is that the bee is carrying pollen to the flowers. But these ideas are connected in a special way. There's a really important word in the sentence that's connecting the ideas. The word *as* at the beginning of the sentence tells me that the two things are happening at the same time.

Mrs. Fabian pulls out another sentence strip and places it under the sentences.

As = At the same time

She has the children read the original sentence with her chorally. Then they read the shorter sentences followed once again by the sentence with the word *as* in it. She models how to unpack another sentence and follows the procedure of thinking aloud as she pulls the shorter sentences from the pocket chart.

CA ELD Standards (Expanding): ELD.PI.1—Contribute to class, group, and partner discussions by listening attentively, following turn-taking rules, and asking and answering questions; ELD.PI.7—Describe the language writers or speakers use to present or support an idea (e.g., the adjectives used to describe people and places) with prompting and moderate support; ELD.PII.6—Combine clauses in an increasing variety of ways to make connections between and to join ideas, for example, to express cause/effect (e.g., She jumped because the dog barked.), in shared language activities guided by the teacher and with increasing independence.

The snapshots and vignettes cited above can be found in their entirety at https://www.cde.ca.gov/ci/rl/cf/, *ELA/ELD Framework*, p. 271.

Notes

Emerging

K No standard for Kindergarten.

1 Condense clauses in simple ways (e.g., changing: *I like blue. I like red. I like purple → I like blue, red, and purple*) to create precise and detailed sentences in shared language activities guided by the teacher and sometimes independently.

2 Condense clauses in simple ways (e.g., changing: *It's green. It's red → It's green and red*) to create precise and detailed sentences in shared language activities guided by the teacher and sometimes independently.

Expanding

K No standard for Kindergarten.

1 Condense clauses in *a growing number* of ways (e.g., *through embedded clauses as in, She's a doctor. She saved the animals. → She's the doctor who saved the animals*) to create precise and detailed sentences in shared language activities guided by the teacher and *with increasing independence.*

2 Condense clauses in *a growing number* of ways (e.g., *through embedded clauses as in, It's a plant. It's found in the rain forest. → It's a green and red plant that's found in the rain forest*) to create precise and detailed sentences *with increasing independence.*

Bridging

K No standard for Kindergarten.

1 Condense clauses in *a variety* of ways (e.g., through embedded clauses and *other condensing, for example, through embedded clauses as in She's a doctor. She's amazing. She saved the animals. → She's the amazing doctor who saved the animals*) to create precise and detailed sentences in shared language activities guided by the teacher and *independently.*

2 Condense clauses in *a variety* of ways (e.g., through embedded clauses and *other condensing, as in, It's a plant. It's green and red. It's found in the tropical rain forest. → It's a green and red plant that's found in the tropical rain forest*) to create precise and detailed sentences *independently.*

Script *in bold italics* indicates content not found in earlier proficiency levels of the same ELD Standard.

Source: *California English Language Development Standards for Grades K–12*, California Department of Education (2012).

Notes

What the **Student** Does

Emerging	Expanding	Bridging
K No standard for Kindergarten.	**K** No standard for Kindergarten.	**K** No standard for Kindergarten.

Gist: *Students condense clauses in a variety of ways to create precise and detailed sentences in shared language activities guided by the teacher and with increasing independence.*

Emerging	Expanding	Bridging
1 They consider:	**1** They *also* consider:	**1** They *also* consider:
• Can I condense clauses to create precise and detailed sentences? • Can I condense ideas when I work with the teacher or by myself?	• Do I know how to use embedded clauses?	• Can I condense ideas when I work by myself?

Gist: *Students condense clauses in a variety of ways to create precise and detailed sentences in shared language activities guided by the teacher and independently.*

Emerging	Expanding	Bridging
2 They consider:	**2** They *also* consider:	**2** They *also* consider:
• Can I condense clauses to create precise and detailed sentences? • Can I condense ideas when I work with the teacher or by myself?	• Do I know how to use embedded clauses?	• Can I condense ideas when I work by myself?

Source: *California English Language Development Standards for Grades K–12 (2012).*

Speaking and Listening Standards	Language Standards
K No standard for Kindergarten.	**K** No standard for Kindergarten.
1 **SL.1.1:** Participate in collaborative conversations with diverse partners about grade 1 topics and texts with peers and adults in small and larger groups. a. Follow agreed-upon rules for discussions (e.g., listening to others with care, speaking one at a time about the topics and texts under discussion). b. Build on others' talk in conversations by responding to the comments of others through multiple exchanges. c. Ask questions to clear up any confusion about the topics and texts under discussion.	**1** **L.1.1:** Demonstrate command of the conventions of standard English grammar and usage when writing or speaking. a. Print all upper- and lowercase letters. b. Use common, proper, and possessive nouns. c. Use singular and plural nouns with matching verbs in basic sentences (e.g., *He hops*; *We hop*). d. Use personal (subject, object), possessive, and indefinite pronouns (e.g., *I*, *me*, *my*; *they*, *them*, *their*; *anyone*, *everything*). e. Use verbs to convey a sense of past, present, and future (e.g., *Yesterday I walked home*; *Today I walk home*; *Tomorrow I will walk home*). f. Use frequently occurring adjectives. g. Use frequently occurring conjunctions (e.g., *and*, *but*, *or*, *so*, *because*). h. Use determiners (e.g., articles, demonstratives). i. Use frequently occurring pre*positions* (e.g., *during*, *beyond*, *toward*). j. Produce and expand complete simple and compound declarative, interrogative, imperative, and exclamatory sentences in response to prompts.
1 **SL.1.4:** Describe people, places, things, and events with relevant details, expressing ideas and feelings clearly. a. Memorize and recide poems, rhymes, and songs with expression.	**1** **L.1.6:** Use words and phrases acquired through conversations, reading and being read to, and responding to texts, including using frequently occurring conjunctions to signal simple relationships (e.g., *because*).
1 **SL.1.6:** Produce complete sentences when appropriate to task and situation. (See grade 1 Language standards 1 and 3 for specific expectations.)	

continued

continued from previous

Speaking and Listening Standards	Language Standards
2 SL.2.4: Tell a story or recount an experience with appropriate facts and relevant, descriptive details, speaking audibly in coherent sentences. a. Plan and deliver a narrative presentation that: recounts a well-elaborated event, includes details, reflects a logical sequence, and provides a conclusion.	**2 L.2.1:** Demonstrate command of the conventions of standard English grammar and usage when writing or speaking. a. Use collective nouns (e.g., *group*). b. Form and use frequently occurring irregular plural nouns (e.g., *feet, children, teeth, mice, fish*). c. Use reflexive pronouns (e.g., *myself, ourselves*). d. Form and use the past tense of frequently occurring irregular verbs (e.g., *sat, hid, told*). e. Use adjectives and adverbs, and choose between them depending on what is to be modified. f. Produce, expand, and rearrange complete simple and compound sentences (e.g., *The boy watched the movie; The little boy watched the movie; The action movie was watched by the little boy*). g. Create readable documents with legible print.
2 SL.2.6: Produce complete sentences when appropriate to task and situation in order to provide requested detail or clarification. (See grade 2 Language standards 1 and 3 for specific expectations.)	**2 L.2.3:** Use knowledge of language and its conventions when writing, speaking, reading, or listening. a. Compare formal and informal uses of English.
	2 L.2.6: Use words and phrases acquired through conversations, reading and being read to, and responding to texts, including using adjectives and adverbs to describe (e.g., *When other kids are happy that makes me happy*).

In addition to the ELA Speaking/Listening and Language standards provided in the chart, Standard 7: Condensing ideas is also linked to ELA Writing standard 1.1–3, 5, and 2.1–3, 5.

Source: *Common Core State Standards, K–12 English Language Arts* (2010).

Notes

What the **Teacher** Does

In order to engage meaningfully with oral and written texts, they continue to build their understanding of how English works (Part II) on a variety of levels: how different text types are organized and structured to achieve particular social purposes, how text can be expanded and enriched using particular language resources, and how ideas can be connected and condensed to convey particular meanings. Importantly, second- and third-grade ELLs deepen their language awareness by analyzing and evaluating the language choices made by writers and speakers and discuss their contributions to meaning (*2014 ELA/ELD* Framework, p. 290).

Teachers can assist students with condensing clauses in a variety of ways to create precise and detailed sentences in shared language activities guided by the teacher and with increasing independence:

- Modeling for students on the board, or with sentence strips, how to condense clauses from familiar texts in order to create precise and detailed sentences.

- Having students circle and underline clauses in familiar texts that have been read as a class, and then with a partner, create more precise and detailed sentences.

- Having students work in partners to condense familiar clauses by using sentence strips that they manipulate to create precise and detailed sentences. For example, changing: *It's green. It's red. It's green and red.*

- Having students work in partners to condense clauses in their own writing. Students can then peer review and provide feedback to their partner regarding using precise and detailed sentences.

- Explaining to students that condensing ideas is important to writers because compression of thoughts and ideas, as well as sentences and sentences, can be a necessity. We also want to leave some details to the imagination of the reader.

- Note: This standard does not appear in kindergarten, as developmentally, students may need assistance with expanding rather than condensing ideas.

Tips for Differentiation by Proficiency Level

- *Emerging*—At the emerging level, the teacher can model how to condense ideas by using sentence strips with familiar text to create precise and detailed sentences. Students can then be given additional sentence strips themselves, and with a partner can work on doing the same.

- *Expanding*—At the expanding level, after the teacher has modeled how to condense ideas in a familiar text, they can have students find additional places in the familiar text where sentences can be combined for precision and detail.

- *Bridging*—At the bridging level, after the teacher has modeled how to condense ideas using a student writing sample, students can work with each other to revise and create precise and detailed sentences.

Source: 2014 ELA/ELD Framework, p. 290.

Academic Vocabulary—Key Words and Phrases Related to Standard 7: Condensing ideas

Clauses: Using a group of words containing a subject and predicate and functioning as a member of a compound sentence but is not a sentence by itself. For example, *"When it rains, I put on my galoshes."*

Condensing ideas: Taking similar ideas in separate sentences and combining them into one sentence that expresses the ideas together. For example, *"I like to play marbles. I like to play hopscotch."* — *"I like to play marbles and hopscotch."*

Embedded clauses: Showing a relationship between the subject of the clause, and the subject of the sentence. For example, *"He is the teacher who gives a pizza party every month."*

Shared language activities: Developing understanding within a team or classroom based on language (e.g., spoken, text, body language, or visuals) in a way that helps them communicate more effectively. This may be simply explaining to another the meaning of a locally used term, or more extensively it may be a level of engagement and interaction that takes months, possibly years to develop.

Simple and compound sentences: Simple sentences contain only one subject and a predicate, but a compound sentence contains more than one subject and more than one predicate.

Source: Taberski & Burke, (2014), *The Common Core Companion: The Standards Decoded, Grades K–2.*

Notes

Example of Practice in Snapshot Related to Standard 7: Condensing ideas

Vignette 3.5. Interactive Read Alouds With Informational Texts Integrated ELA, Literacy, and Science Instruction in Grade 1

Mrs. Fabian works with her students during designated ELD time to unpack sentences in other science texts she is using, focusing strategically on the aspects of the sentences that make them dense (e.g., long noun phrases, prepositional phrases). She uses a rubric based on the CA ELD Standards to assess how individual students are progressing with their use of particular language resources (e.g., vocabulary, grammatical structures, text organization). Whenever possible, she encourages them to use the new language, prompting them with questions like, *"How can you combine [or condense] those two ideas to show they are happening at the same time?"* Although the children often produce imperfect sentences, Mrs. Fabian offers corrective feedback sparingly since she knows that the children are experimenting with language and practicing the grammatical structures that they will continue to learn as the unit progresses.

Primary CA CCSS for ELA/Literacy: RI.1.2—Identify the main topic and retell key details of a text; RI.1.3—Describe the connection between two individuals, events, ideas, or pieces of information in a text; RI.1.7—Use the illustrations and details in a text to describe its key ideas; W.1.7—Participate in shared research and writing projects . . . ; SL.1.1—Participate in collaborative conversations with diverse partners; SL.1.2—Ask and answer questions about key details in a text read aloud . . . ; L.1.6—Use words and phrases acquired through conversations, reading and being read to, and responding to texts . . .

CA ELD Standards (Expanding): ELD.PI.1—Contribute to class, group, and partner discussions by listening attentively, following turn-taking rules, and asking and answering questions; ELD.PI.5—Demonstrate active listening to read-alouds and oral presentations by asking and answering questions with oral sentence frames and occasional prompting and support; ELD.PI.11—Offer opinions and provide good reasons and some textual evidence or relevant background knowledge (e.g., paraphrased examples from text or knowledge of content); ELD.PI.12b—Use a growing number of general academic and domain-specific words . . .

The snapshots and vignettes cited above can be found in their entirety at https://www.cde.ca.gov/ci/rl/cf/, *ELA/ELD Framework,* p. 263.

Notes

Notes

Notes

Notes

Notes

Notes

Notes

Notes

CORWIN
A SAGE Publishing Company

Helping educators make the greatest impact

CORWIN HAS ONE MISSION: to enhance education through intentional professional learning.

We build long-term relationships with our authors, educators, clients, and associations who partner with us to develop and continuously improve the best evidence-based practices that establish and support lifelong learning.